Maman & Me

Maman & Me

Recipes from Our Iranian American Family

ROYA SHARIAT AND **GITA SADEH**

Photographs by Farrah Skeiky

PA PRESS

PRINCETON ARCHITECTURAL PRESS · NEW YORK

PUBLISHED BY
Princeton Architectural Press
A division of Chronicle Books LLC
70 West 36th Street, New York, NY 10018
www.papress.com

© 2023 Roya Shariat
Photographs © 2023 Farrah Skeiky
All rights reserved.
Printed and bound in China
26 25 24 23   4 3 2 1 First edition

EDITOR: Holly La Due
DESIGNER: Paul Wagner
TYPESETTING: Natalie Snodgrass

LIBRARY OF CONGRESS CATALOGING-IN-PUBLICATION DATA
Names: Shariat, Roya, 1992– author. | Sadeh, Gita, 1956– author.
Title: Maman and me : recipes from our Iranian American family / Roya Shariat and Gita Sadeh.
Description: New York : Princeton Architectural Press, 2023. |
Includes index. | Summary: "Delicious home-cooked Iranian American recipes
from the mother-and-daughter duo Gita Sadeh and Roya Shariat" —Provided by publisher.
Identifiers: LCCN 2022057144 | ISBN 9781797223643 (hardcover) | ISBN 9781797227009 (ebook)
Subjects: LCSH: Cooking, Iranian. | Cooking, American. | LCGFT: Cookbooks.
Classification: LCC TX725.17 S443 2023 | DDC 641.5955—dc23/eng/20221202
LC record available at https://lccn.loc.gov/2022057144

Contents

This book is a tribute to all the immigrant
parents and caretakers who left their homes for
a foreign land, keeping their loved ones nourished
and cared for through food.

Maman and Baba, this one's for you.

سپاسگزارم

Introduction

Maman and Me is a cookbook celebrating the beautiful nuances of Iranian American cuisine. It's a story of food across borders—how, like us, it evolves, assimilates, and sometimes transforms completely.

This book is focused on the *here*, *now*, and *how*—the recipes, adaptations, techniques, kitchen hacks, and resources we use to make food that tastes like home. Home is not a static, monolithic concept or a literal place. As clichéd as it sounds, home is within all of us, changing all the time.

You might be wondering what makes this book Iranian American, or what that term means. The recipes in this book paint a picture that is both Iranian and American, and the sum of those two identities. We are writing the recipes and stories that reflect our lived experience—*me* growing up in this country, and *Maman* moving to this country at the very age I am while writing this book.

Migration inevitably influences many aspects of our lives, and one particularly visible place is in the kitchen. We notice this almost daily, whether we're using a coffee grinder to grind saffron or discovering that wonton wrappers make the best sambusas. You'll notice this while reading and preparing recipes from this book. Recipes like Orange and Cardamom French Toast (page 39), Tortilla Tahdig (page 107), Pomegranate Molasses Spritz (page 173), and Maman's Peach Muffins (page 183) are just a few examples of the unique cultural milieu this cookbook is rooted in.

This book is a love letter to Iranian people, and to our cuisine that so beautifully exemplifies our resilience. There is so much care and tenderness in Iranian cuisine: the steady simmering of stews until each flavor melds together perfectly, the verdant greens at the center of every meal, the fork-tender eggplants and meats braised over time, the crunch of nuts and the sweetness of raisins strewn throughout a pilaf, the tartness of limes, the scent of saffron wafting through the air. As you'll see in this book, Iranian cooking is bright and unexpected, full of vegetables, herbs, and sweet and savory spices.

Our food is meant to be shared with the people you love. There is joy in assembling a massive breakfast board with warm bread, fresh herbs, and feta, then watching your friends dive in with their hands. There is no greater pleasure than flipping over a tahdig, seeing that it isn't burnt, and making that first crisp, audible incision while your guests gasp and gawk over it. Preparing chai, with some sweets and a platter of cut fruit to accompany it, is how we say, "I love you," "I'm sorry," and "thank you."

Maman and Me is just as much an Iranian cookbook as it is an American cookbook. While the dishes in this book might not have been on your table growing up, we hope they make it into your regular rotation. Some of them are easy riffs on classics, such as an egg and tomato omelet (Omlet, page 24), while others are more complex, including a spicy and sour tamarind fish stew (Ghalieh Mahi, page 144). I think you'll be surprised at how accessible and simple many of these recipes are—they look harder than they seem, I promise! Regardless of what your background or cooking experience might be, we hope these dishes make you feel at home in every sense.

Our cooking techniques, ingredients, and recipes can tell us a lot about who we are, what we care about, and how we gather. For many of us in diaspora communities, food is synonymous with home. Maman and many immigrant caretakers everywhere use cooking to keep the memories of home alive, and as a tool to pass on important pieces of their heritage to a new generation. Food is the lifeline that keeps us tethered to the motherland and the thing that gives us comfort, joy, and relief. It's a core part of our identity.

Food and recipes, like art and literature, are cultural markers and pieces of history. Writing this book is an act of keeping recipes alive, and through this process I hope to also immortalize the people, stories, and culture behind them. Recipes aren't created in a vacuum—whether it's my great-grandmother's Noon Masti (page 192), Maman's Creamy Leek and Potato Soup with Turmeric and Carrots (page 90), or my late friend Mona's Hazelnut Tahini Rolls (page 199), the people behind recipes are just as important as the recipes themselves.

Speaking of people, I should tell you a bit about Maman. Maman is a teacher: She teaches preschoolers during the week and spends her weekends tutoring kids and adults in Farsi, and she will teach anyone in her immediate vicinity something worth knowing—whether that's how to make tahdig or which days the local TJ Maxx gets new inventory. Maman self-identifies as a "lifelong learner" and is constantly seeking out new information to expand her knowledge. Her interest in cooking began at a young age, and by the time she was in her twenties, she became a savvy cook highly regarded by friends, family, and even random acquaintances, who hoped for an invite to one of her mehmoonis (dinner parties).

After moving to the United States in the eighties, Maman, like most immigrants, experienced a slew of challenges and setbacks. Disrupting your entire life to migrate and make a new one elsewhere involves countless changes and requires constant adjustments. Among the many challenges she faced was how to preserve her culture and pass it on to her family. Sharing her cooking and food felt like one of the clearest and best ways to do so, but recreating Iranian cuisine in an entirely new country came to be its own massive obstacle. I'm in awe of Maman's culinary grit and talent, her conviction that a recipe is never finished, and her ability to make even a dish like shrimp scampi taste Iranian. She can find the most stunning serving platter for any item of food, from a side of pickles to a tray of salmon, whether this is for a simple lunch at home or when hosting thirty of her friends. You'll see that talent and creativity throughout this book: Every piece of kitchenware and all the tablecloths photographed are from Maman's personal collection, accrued throughout her life. She also has the uncanny ability to find the perfect size container for *any* amount of leftovers, possessing a level of spatial awareness that I'll spend the rest of my life trying to understand. And most importantly, she has the generous heart and genuine kindness to make anyone feel at home in her presence, especially in her kitchen.

Cooking Iranian food in America is a lot easier and more accessible nowadays than it was thirty, or even ten, years ago. Finding stores that sold the ingredients we sought was a constant challenge, so we began to innovate. After all, immigrants are innovators, even if not always by choice. With this cookbook, we hope to celebrate cooking Iranian food in the diaspora, with recipes that bring all the flavor but eschew some tradition for innovation.

I'd be remiss to say that this book is only about finding comfort and joy. It's also about fear and alleviating that fear. It's rooted in my ever-present fear of losing my parents. The fear my parents have about not passing on enough of their own culture, stories, and traditions. The fear all of us carry about losing our heritage and connection to "home" as we grow older. My fear of not being able to perfectly replicate the incredible cooking I was raised with—that my cooking (and I) will never be good enough. Collecting these recipes and writing this book is one way I'm tackling this fear head-on and cementing this piece of my history. If you've ever felt similarly, I hope this book resonates with you, and I hope you find your way to immortalize whatever home means to you.

We hope these recipes and stories bring you joy and nourishment and expand your perspective on what Iranian American cuisine looks—and tastes—like.

Notes on Language

The choice of whether to use the word *Iranian* versus *Persian* can carry political implications. I choose to use *Iranian* throughout this book, because people living inside Iran have always referred to their country as Iran.

You'll see the term *Southwest Asian* sprinkled throughout this book, almost entirely in reference to specialty grocers where you can find specific ingredients needed for some of the recipes. *Southwest Asia* refers to the region of the world that Iran is in, and it's also a term that doesn't carry the colonialist and orientalist origins of *Middle East*.

The term *Middle East* was coined by British imperialists who devised it because the region is in the "middle" and "east" of Europe. There's no official consensus or designation for which countries are even part of the Middle East, which is a vast region of the world. I prefer the term *Southwest Asia* given that it's rooted in geography rather than a political view. This is a relatively new term, but language matters. I'm eager and hopeful to see a broader linguistic shift toward this term.

And now, some language lessons:
Farsi is an extremely poetic language full of creative and fun idioms that have no English equivalent. There are food-related terms that feel essential to enjoying and understanding our food culture, so we're sharing a few of our favorites with you.

The words for *kitchen* and *chef* are *ashpazkhaneh* and *ashpaz*, which literally translate to "place to cook ash" and "person who cooks ash," respectively. Ash is now known as our iconic bean soup, but back in the day, many dishes—including rice—were called *ash*.

The word for *heart* and *stomach* are one and the same in Farsi: *del*. I can't think of anything else that so succinctly demonstrates how critical food is in Iranian culture.

The word *loqme* (pronounced loghmeh) can refer to a morsel of food or a little bite, but it also signifies a perfect bite: a piece of food that has all the right components, wrapped in a piece of bread. For example, at breakfast, a handful of warm lavash bread sandwiched with fresh herbs, a walnut, and a cube of feta would be a loqme.

When we're eating soup, we tear up slices of flatbread and toss them into the bowl as we start eating it. The bread chunks become soggy and soft over time, adding texture and heartiness to the broth. There's a word for this very activity: *tilit*.

The phrase *ja oftadeh* translates to "fell into place," and it means when a dish is ready. This typically is used in the context of soups and stews, which need time to slowly simmer and set, thickening up with the distinct flavors melding together just right. You can cook any of the stews in this cookbook for hours and they'll only get better with time.

A common way to show affection is to use the phrase *jeegaret ra bekhoram*, which literally translates to "I will eat your liver."

Befarmayeed means "go ahead" or "after you." Any time you're eating in someone's house, they'll say this to usher you into your seat and start eating.

Bah bah doesn't really have a translation. It is a sound we make when we see, smell, or eat delicious food.

Noosh e jaan is our version of *bon appétit*, but in typical Iranian fashion, much more dramatic. The phrase translates to "may it nourish your soul."

The phrase *az sir ta piaz* literally translates to "from garlic to onion," but it really means from A to Z.

To show how you might use some of these phrases in practice: If you're hosting friends for dinner, you can invite them to the ashpazkhaneh for a loqme of something while you're finalizing the meal. If they have a cute child or pet with them, you can say, "jeegaret ra bekhoram!" When food is ready and you'd like people to get seated, you can say, "befarmayeed." Your guests might say, "bah bah," upon seeing the delicious spread. When they thank you for cooking such an incredible Iranian meal (using the recipes from this book, of course), you'll say, "noosh e jaan."

Finally, you'll need to understand the word, and the cultural phenomenon, of *taarof*. Taarof is a form of ritual politeness prevalent in Iranian culture. In social situations, it's crucial to show respect and deference. Taarof might look like offering to pay the bill at a restaurant, it might mean inviting a guest over who stays in your bed while you sleep on the couch, or it might mean you offer chai to your guests a few times, insisting they must try it even if they're full or say no.

Now, before this turns into a language book, befarmayeed into our pantry...

Key to Abbreviations

VEG – Vegetarian   **VGN** – Vegan   **GF** – Gluten-Free

Pantry

Maman's pantry might be one of the best manifestations of *Maman and Me* in real life. The pantry is the size of a walk-in closet, with shelves full of spices, sauces, dried herbs, and pastes and ingredients ranging from mint she dries in the microwave to egg noodles for beef stroganoff to adobo seasoning to homemade pickles. My pantry, on the other hand, is one small cabinet in a Brooklyn apartment. Regardless of your pantry situation, you'll be relieved to know that Iranian cuisine is reliant on just a few staple spices used in different ways. Once you have those ingredients in your kitchen, you'll be able to cook most of the dishes in this book (and then some).

 This list is comprehensive, so don't get intimidated: Starting with just the dried herbs is more than enough; everything else is a nice to have. A few online retailers that carry most of these ingredients are Kalustyan's, Sadaf, Mideast Grocers, and Diaspora Co. (particularly for spices).

Salt

Maman's go-to is Morton's table salt, which is fine salt, while mine is Diamond Crystal kosher salt. Morton's is more easily accessible in most grocers, so we developed these recipes using it. It's important to know that Morton's table salt is saltier than other varieties, which is actually a good thing if you're using a different variety! Under salting is always fixable, so taste the recipes as you make them and add more salt to your liking. I like using Diamond Crystal kosher salt because it's more forgiving: I can be generous with a pour and not worry about overdoing it.

Black Pepper

We typically have two types of black pepper on hand: ground black pepper in a jar with a spoon and a grinder with fresh black pepper. We use the latter to finish dishes, in salads and cold dishes, and on meat-centric dishes. For most soups and stews, we're using ground black pepper, which goes perfectly with the next ingredient…

Ground Turmeric

Turmeric is rich, floral, and fragrant, and an essential ingredient in many Iranian recipes. It adds a vibrant yellow hue to anything it touches—including your skin and countertops, so be careful with it! The active compound in turmeric is curcumin, which is widely reported to have health benefits. However, curcumin is best absorbed by our bodies when turmeric is combined with black pepper. We'll generally add turmeric and black pepper to recipes at the same time for this reason. Additionally, turmeric is fat-soluble (your body digests it best when it's in oil), so we almost always add it to a recipe along with oil.

Saffron

Grown widely in Iran and Afghanistan, saffron is the dried stigma of the purple crocus flower. The process of harvesting saffron is incredibly laborious. It takes hundreds of individual hand-picked flowers to produce a commercially viable amount of saffron, which makes it an expensive spice. Because saffron is so precious, you want to be sure you're using it properly. We keep saffron threads in the refrigerator, grind them into a powder with a mortar and pestle the day we want to use them, and then bloom them in liquid. If you're having trouble grinding, you can always add a pinch of sugar to smooth the process. You have two options to bloom saffron: hot or cold! With the hot method, you add a few tablespoons of boiled water that has had a minute or so to cool to the ground saffron in a small cup or bowl and let the powder steep into a beautiful, amber liquid for 10 to 15 minutes before adding it to a dish. The cold method involves sprinkling ground saffron over a few ice cubes in a small cup or bowl and waiting 20 to 30 minutes for the ice to melt and get that same golden liquid. Iran produces more than 90 percent of the world's saffron, although it's harder to come by in the United States. Saharkhiz Saffron is a wonderful Iranian saffron brand that can be purchased through the online retailer Tavazo. Moonflowers and Diaspora Co. produce great saffron from Afghanistan and Kashmir, respectively, which are sold online.

Ground Cumin

Cumin is earthy, warm, and rounds out the flavors of a dish when used in small quantities. It's easy to find in most grocery stores and is also used in many South Asian and Latin American dishes.

Curry Powder

Curry powder is not a single spice, but rather a blend of several different spices that usually includes turmeric, black pepper, ginger, cardamom, fenugreek, and cinnamon. It's a rich blend that adds depth to any stew or dish, without overpowering it through a single spice. It might seem redundant that we use it alongside turmeric and cinnamon, but the combination of spices produces a distinct flavor that we love to use in certain dishes for an extra punch.

Ground Cinnamon and Cinnamon Sticks

Cinnamon is a versatile ingredient that adds warmth and richness to savory dishes. Cinnamon sticks are great for stews and braises: You can add one to the cooking liquid and let it simmer along with the ingredients, lending aroma and flavor to the final dish.

Cardamom

Cardamom lends a fruity, warming spice to both sweet and savory dishes. We always have green cardamom pods on hand, which we smash with the back of a knife, discarding the husk, and then grind in a mortar and pestle to create a powder. We also love to use whole pods when brewing coffee or tea, adding three pods to our teakettle (one for an individual serving would be sufficient).

Sumac

Sumac is a stellar pantry staple that we find ourselves using more than any recipe ever calls for. This beautiful red powder tastes like bright citrus, spicing up anything from plain white rice to salad dressing to cocktails, such as the Sumac Smash (page 174)!

Dried Lime (Limoo Omani)

Dried limes are a specialty ingredient easily found at Southwest Asian grocers and online. These limes are dried out in the sun and lend a punch of acidity and a touch of earthy bitterness to stews and soups. You can find the limes whole (our preference) or ground into a powder. In a stew that calls for limoo omani, we'll simmer the lime until it's soft and rehydrated, and eat it alongside the stew, being mindful not to eat the seeds. It is incredibly sour and mouth-puckering, but that's one of the delights of cooking Iranian food—we love acidity!

Dried Herbs

You'll see a few dried herbs in these recipes that you might not already have in your spice cabinet, mainly dried mint, dill, and fenugreek. For mint and dill, you can always start with fresh herbs and dehydrate them in the microwave: Put the fresh herbs on a plate and microwave them in 30-second intervals, tossing and turning them after each round. Once the herbs feel sufficiently dried and aren't burnt, you can crush them with a mortar and pestle, or with your hands. Fenugreek is readily available online and in South Asian and Southwest Asian grocers. It has a distinct bitterness that's hard to replicate, so we recommend keeping it on hand.

Tamarind Paste

This isn't a *must*, because we use it in a tiny number of recipes, but it's great to have in the pantry and to experiment with in your cooking. Tamarind paste tastes sour, tart, bright, and almost citrusy, and it's a versatile ingredient that you can use to make salad dressings, dipping sauces, marinades, and more. Tamarind paste is easily found at South Asian grocers, and I recommend going with the jarred variety, which is easier to use than a brick of paste with seeds in it.

Rosewater

Rosewater is the beautiful, fragrant distillation of rose petals in water. Rosewater has sweet and savory uses and can even be used as a facial toner. Our go-to brand is Cortas, which can be found in most Southwest Asian grocers and online.

Dried Rose Petals

Dried rose petals and dried whole roses are a nice luxury to have. They add aroma and color to teas, yogurt dishes, and desserts, but aren't a must for any of our recipes.

Pomegranate Molasses

Rich, sweet, and tart, this syrupy liquid is jam-packed with flavor, and will add complexity to drinks, stews, salads, dips, meats, and more. Experimentation with it will yield amazing results: Try it in a marinade, as a glaze for meat, or stir a spoonful into your seltzer and you'll be pleasantly surprised. Our favorite brand is Cortas, readily found in Southwest Asian grocers and online.

Orange-Blossom Water

Only one recipe in this book calls for orange-blossom water (which is sometimes called orange-flower water), so it's not a must by any means, just another nice floral ingredient to experiment with in sweet and savory dishes.

Rice

Rice is life! Iranian rice dishes are mostly made with basmati rice, a fragrant, long-grain rice grown widely across South Asia. Basmati rice holds up to longer cooking, doesn't clump together, and creates the beautiful tahdig we strive to make with every rice dish. We love Aahu Barah brand, but whatever kind you can find in your local grocer should work wonderfully.

Dried Fruits

There are a few dried fruits you'll see throughout this cookbook and across Iranian cuisine. We make several pilafs with both black and golden raisins, which we always keep on hand, plumping them with oil and spices. Dates are on our sofrehs (spreads) all the time as a snack and source of sweetness and are our favorite way to break the fast during Ramadan! You'll also see them in pilafs in this book. Finally, dried barberries (zereshk) are beautiful red berries that add a burst of sourness and brightness to rice dishes, even just regular white rice. Barberries can be found in most Southwest Asian grocers and online and need to be rehydrated and fried in oil or butter before consuming. We typically keep prepared barberries in a sealed container in the refrigerator, so they're always ready to go.

Fresh Herbs (Sabzi)

There is always a heaping platter of fresh herbs at the table. It's believed that fresh herbs help you digest rich, hearty meals and have health benefits. We tend to buy herbs in large sizes from East Asian grocers, washing and drying them all at once, and keep them in the refrigerator in sealed containers or bags with a damp paper towel, which keeps them fresh for more than a week. Our favorites are cilantro, parsley, mint, multiple varieties of basil, dill, green onions, French tarragon, chives, and radishes (radishes are always grouped together with herbs, but we have no clue why!).

Nuts

Nuts are yet another Iranian table staple. My parents grew up picking and eating fresh walnuts and almonds off the tree, and the closest they have gotten to that in the United States is soaking nuts whole. We buy whole unroasted almonds and walnuts, wash them with warm water first, rinse

them in a few changes of cold water, then place them in a container with cold water and leave them in the refrigerator. The next morning, the nuts are ready to go! The nuts taste softer and sweeter, and their skins slide off easily thanks to the soaking. We change the soaking water nightly throughout the course of the week. For cooking, we also love to include slivered pistachios and almonds in rice pilafs.

Bread

Bread is always at the breakfast table, and served alongside soups, as well as some of our favorite mezze dips. There are many incredible varieties of Iranian bread. A few popular varieties you can find Stateside are barbari, lavash, sangak, and taftoon. These are all flatbreads, some leavened and some not. I recommend looking into Iranian or Southwest Asian bakeries in your area to try some fresh ones, or even making them yourself if you like baking bread. They aren't the most complex to make and are such fantastic pairings for our dishes.

Dairy

Iranian cuisine is not heavy on dairy, except for a few key ingredients. We love thick yogurt and labneh by the spoonful, next to rice pilafs, in our soups, and to dip chips in. Feta is our go-to cheese, always at the breakfast table or on a mezze platter. Kashk is a fermented dairy product, often labeled as "whey" Stateside, that is a salty, savory, umami bomb. It's used in a small number of recipes here, but it's fun and versatile to play with in all sorts of cooking.

Tea (Chai)

Tea is an integral part of Iranian culture, and it is our drink of choice from dusk till dawn. It's always made with black tea and served in glass cups so you can see the strength of the brew—a rich, dark, ruby red is ideal. Maman makes a tea blend from several different store varieties (naturally), which she places in a massive container that was originally a tub of pretzels. She purchases a box of each of the following: Ahmad Tea's Cardamom Tea, Ahmad Tea's Special Blend, Shah Abbasi's Earl Grey, Sadaf's Special Blend with Cardamom, and Sadaf's Mélange Special with Earl Grey. Any one of these tea blends would be sufficient, and you can jazz up your cup with one or two whole green cardamom pods per person. If you can get your hands on crystal sugar at a Southwest Asian grocer (bonus points if you get the saffron variety), try that with your tea for a sweet treat that we believe cures all ailments, from cramps to heartsickness.

A Note on Blanching Meat

It's not uncommon in Southwest Asian, South Asian, or East Asian kitchens to boil red meat in water for several minutes before cooking it in a soup or stew, discarding the cloudy water afterward. Home cooks believe this can help remove any bad smells or impurities from the meat, as well as some gaminess, resulting in a better final dish. I don't always do this, but you'll see this step included in recipes if you want to give it a try.

Breakfast

Morning Herb and Cheese Platter (Noon Paneer Sabzi)

VEG — 23

Classic Omelet (Omlet)

VEG · GF — 24

Sweet Date Omelet (Gheysavah)

VEG · GF — 27

Hot Dog Scramble (Sosees Tokmemorgh)

GF — 28

Sweet or Savory Labneh Toast

VEG — 31

Figgy Toast

VEG — 32

Orange-Blossom Yogurt Parfait

VEG · GF — 35

Carrot Jam (Moraba Havij)

VEG · GF — 36

Orange and Cardamom French Toast

VEG — 39

Rosy Pancakes

VEG — 40

Turkey Porridge, Two Ways (Halim)

MORNING HERB AND CHEESE PLATTER (NOON PANEER SABZI) VEG

You'll find this platter on our tables all day long, most often at breakfast. Herbs and cheese are a perfect pairing for most foods—this platter goes just as well with hot tea and omelets as it does with white wine and mezze. It also requires no cooking. Think of it as a breakfast charcuterie board, swapping meats for something lighter. The best way to make this is to choose your own adventure. For those who aren't used to eating raw herbs, fill the platter with herbs you generally like as a starting point. Rinsing and soaking the nuts takes away some of the bitterness, making them softer and buttery, just like fresh nuts off the tree.

Serves 5

—

¼ cup (55 g) unsalted butter

One 8 oz (230 g) block feta cheese

One 4 oz (115 g) log goat cheese

1 pint (340 g) cherry tomatoes

3 Persian cucumbers, quartered or diced

8 oz (230 g) red or green grapes

½ cup (60 g) walnuts, rinsed in warm water then soaked in cold water for at least 2 hours (preferably overnight)

½ cup (70 g) almonds, rinsed in warm water then soaked in cold water for at least 2 hours (preferably overnight)

ANY COMBINATION OF THE FOLLOWING:

1 small bunch fresh flat-leaf parsley

1 small bunch fresh cilantro

1 small bunch fresh mint

1 small bunch fresh basil

1 small bunch fresh dill

1 small bunch fresh tarragon

1 small bunch green onions, green ends thinly sliced and bloomed in ice water for 15 minutes

1 small bunch radishes, thinly sliced or cut into roses and bloomed in ice water for 15 minutes

1 tsp black caraway seeds, for sprinkling on goat cheese (optional)

Warm lavash or pita bread, for serving

On a large serving tray or cutting board, assemble your butter, cheeses, vegetables, fruit, nuts, and herbs as you would a meat and cheese plate. We try to group different items together, which creates a lovely color contrast: Pairing the herbs beside the nuts, or the cheeses next to the grapes, looks striking and allows people to make their own flavor combinations. We sprinkle black caraway seeds on our goat cheese, so it stands apart from the feta. Place warm bread alongside the herbs, then make your loqme (perfect bite) using whatever mix of flavors and ingredients look best to you!

If you have leftover herbs, the best way to store them is in an airtight bag with a damp paper towel to keep them moist and fresh for up to 1 week. You can keep the nuts soaked in the refrigerator for up to 1 week.

CLASSIC OMELET (OMLET) VEG · GF

This omelet is an everyday breakfast staple in most Iranian households. Technically speaking, it's not actually an omelet (it's more of a scramble), but for some reason the Farsi word for this dish is just *omlet*. This recipe is easy and endlessly modifiable. The general ratio here is to use two eggs and one tomato per person, which you can scale up to feed a crowd. You can add onions and garlic, use canned tomatoes instead of fresh, keep the eggs whole instead of whisking, add spices to the mixture, and so on. Adding tomato paste punches up the tomato flavor, but it's completely optional. We love this dish in its simplest, purest form, which we make at least once a week for breakfast, and often when we're too tired to make dinner.

Serves 2

———

1 Tbsp extra-virgin olive oil

2 Roma tomatoes, roughly chopped

Fine salt and freshly ground black pepper

4 large eggs

1 Tbsp tomato paste (optional)

Feta cheese, for garnish (optional)

Lavash or flatbread, warm, for serving (optional)

In a medium sauté pan over medium-high heat, warm the oil until glistening. Add the chopped tomatoes and sprinkle with salt and pepper. Cook, using a spatula to occasionally move the tomatoes around in the pan, for 5 minutes.

While the tomatoes cook down, crack the eggs into a small bowl and whisk them until the mixture is uniform in color and texture, and is light and foamy.

Once the tomatoes are softened and their liquid is mostly evaporated, stir in the tomato paste (if using) and let it cook for 2 minutes, or until it has slightly darkened in color. Otherwise, add the eggs, along with salt and black pepper. Cook for 3 to 5 minutes, pushing the mixture around in the pan so the eggs can form small curds and taking occasional breaks in between to let the eggs set. Remove the eggs from the heat while they're still slightly wet and glistening.

Sprinkle the omelet with feta, if desired, and serve with warm bread (if using).

SWEET DATE OMELET (GHEYSAVAH) VEG · GF

This sweet omelet is an ideal breakfast before a big hike or moments when you need lasting sustenance. Sweet eggs might sound unusual, but the result tastes custardy, caramelly, and rich, with flavors reminiscent of French toast. We sizzle dates in melted butter until they're warmed through and caramelized and pour in whisked eggs to complete the dish. It's a simple, unexpected combination that magically turns into a warming breakfast that will make you feel cozy and satisfied.

Serves 2

———

2 Tbsp unsalted butter

5 Medjool dates,
   halved and pitted

4 large eggs

Fine salt

Ground cinnamon,
   for sprinkling

Honey, for drizzling
   (optional)

In a medium nonstick frying pan (with a lid) over medium heat, melt the butter, swirling the pan to evenly coat the bottom. Add the pitted dates, placing them cut-side down in the pan. Let the dates cook for 2 minutes, then flip them and cook for 2 more minutes, or until they're slightly softened.

While the dates are caramelizing, crack the eggs into a small bowl and whisk them until the mixture is uniform in color and texture, and is light and foamy.

Once the dates are caramelized, pour the eggs into the pan and sprinkle with a pinch of salt. Leave the eggs untouched for 1 to 2 minutes while the bottom sets. Cover and continue cooking for 3 to 5 minutes, or until the top of the eggs is just set. Sprinkle a dash of cinnamon over the top and remove the pan from the heat.

Serve the omelet warm, with a drizzle of honey, if desired.

HOT DOG SCRAMBLE (SOSEES TOKMEMORGH) GF

This is the Iranian take on sausage and eggs. Instead of using actual sausages and cooking them separately, we use hot dogs and cook them with the eggs. This scramble is comfort food at its best, and like most of our breakfast dishes, is suitable to eat any time of day. I usually make this when I'm stressed or when there's little left in the refrigerator, sometimes eating it over rice with hot sauce. It is sublime nestled into a loqme (perfect bite) with warm bread.

Serves 2

——

1 Tbsp extra-virgin olive oil

2 beef hot dogs, cut
    into ½ in (13 mm)
    thick rounds

4 large eggs

Fine salt and freshly ground
    black pepper

Lavash or flatbread, warm,
    for serving (optional)

In a medium sauté pan over medium-high heat, warm the oil until glistening. Add the hot dogs and cook, turning occasionally, for about 5 minutes, or until they are lightly crisp and browned.

While the hot dogs cook, crack the eggs into a small bowl and whisk them until the mixture is uniform in color and texture, and is light and foamy.

Once the hot dogs are browned, pour the eggs into the pan. Add a small pinch of salt and pepper—hot dogs are already salty, so it's better to start with less and add more once the dish is complete. Push the eggs around slowly to form medium curds, taking breaks to allow them to set. Remove the pan from the heat once the eggs are set but lightly glistening.

Serve with warm bread (if using).

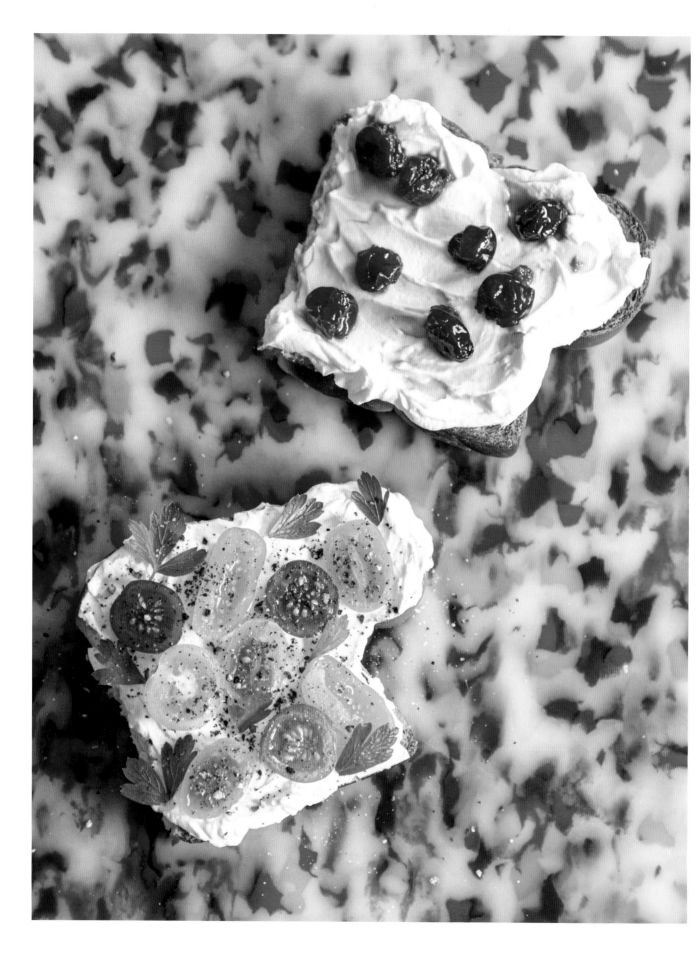

SWEET OR SAVORY LABNEH TOAST VEG

Labneh is thick, strained yogurt, which has a beautiful spreadable consistency suitable for a wide range of dishes. This recipe is entirely up to you, depending on what you're craving! Labneh toast is delicious in both sweet and savory form. We're giving you one option for each, but feel free to get creative with anything in your pantry—we love using smoked salmon, za'atar, pomegranate molasses, fresh fruit, and even granola on our labneh toasts.

Serves 1

———

SAVORY TOAST

1 slice any bread, including bagels and English muffins, toasted

1 to 2 Tbsp labneh

¼ cup (40 g) cherry tomatoes, halved

1 Tbsp finely chopped fresh flat-leaf parsley

Flaky sea salt and freshly ground black pepper

Sumac, for garnish (optional)

SWEET TOAST

1 slice any bread, including bagels and English muffins, toasted

1 to 2 Tbsp labneh

1 to 2 tsp any fruit jam/ preserves

Flaky sea salt

To make the savory toast:
Place the warm toasted bread on a serving plate and spoon the labneh on top. Spread the labneh with the back of a spoon until the bread is evenly covered with a thick layer. Place the cherry tomatoes on top and sprinkle the parsley all over the toast. Sprinkle with salt, pepper, and a dusting of sumac, if desired.

To make the sweet toast:
Place the warm toasted bread on a serving plate and spoon the labneh on top. Spread the labneh with the back of a spoon until the bread is evenly covered with a thick layer. Using a clean spoon, pour fruit jam on top and lightly spread it with the back of a spoon so the jam layer is covering the labneh. Sprinkle lightly with salt to make the sweet and savory flavors pop.

FIGGY TOAST VEG

Figs are an incredibly special fruit that feel like a gift every summer. In the Northeast region of the United States, where I live, figs are typically in season from August through October, so that's the best time of year to eat them. Figs are ripe when their exterior is lightly squeezable and soft, and their insides are jammy. In this recipe, I treat figs just like jam, and make my favorite version of a peanut butter and jelly sandwich.

Serves 1
—

1 slice brioche, challah,
    or shokupan (Japanese
    milk bread), toasted
2 Tbsp peanut butter or
    other nut butter
3 to 5 fresh figs, halved
    or quartered
Flaky sea salt

Place the warm toasted bread on a serving plate, and spread the peanut butter on top. Take the figs and place them, skin-side down, evenly across the bread. If the figs are very ripe and soft, you can lightly smash them with the back of a spoon to get some of their flesh directly on the bread. Sprinkle with salt and enjoy.

ORANGE-BLOSSOM YOGURT PARFAIT VEG · GF

Orange-blossom water is an extract distilled from the flowers of bitter orange trees. Much like rosewater, it's quite fragrant and can take both sweet and savory dishes (and drinks!) to the next level. After getting bored of my typical yogurt bowls, I started experimenting and landed on a sublime combination. Orange-blossom water perks up a basic breakfast staple and turns it into something special.

Serves 1

——

5 oz (140 g) Greek yogurt

3 Tbsp coarsely chopped walnuts

½ tsp orange-blossom water

1 apple, finely chopped

Honey, for drizzling

Flaky sea salt

Pour the Greek yogurt into a small bowl. Stir in the walnuts and orange-blossom water. Top with the apple, a drizzle of honey, and some salt. Enjoy!

CARROT JAM (MORABA HAVIJ) VEG · GF

On any Iranian breakfast spread, you'll typically find at least one variety of delicious, unique jam, which goes beautifully with flatbread, butter, and salty feta. Moraba havij is a standout, consisting of sweet carrot preserves, scented with cardamom and rose and spiked with nuts for color and crunch. I love it on buttered bread or by the spoonful. This is a versatile jam that can be used to top a cake or other baked goods or added to rice pilafs for sweetness—see page 121 for our jeweled rice that features this gorgeous spread. If you can't find shredded carrots, grate about 8 medium carrots on the large holes of a box grater.

Makes 2 (8 oz / 230 g) jars

———

**Two 10 oz (285 g) packages
   shredded carrots**

**2 cups (400 g) granulated
   sugar**

**6 whole cardamom pods,
   preferably wrapped
   in cheesecloth or an
   herb sachet**

⅓ cup (35 g) slivered almonds

1 tsp fresh lemon juice

2 Tbsp rosewater

**Generous pinch of ground
   saffron, bloomed in
   2 Tbsp hot water**

**3 Tbsp slivered pistachios,
   soaked in ¼ cup (60 ml)
   rosewater (optional)**

**Flatbread and butter,
   for serving**

Place the shredded carrots and sugar in a medium pot and stir to combine. Cover with 6 cups (1.4 L) of water and bring to a boil over high heat. Once the mixture is boiling, skim any foam from the top and add the cardamom pods. Stir the mixture, then turn the heat to medium-high and simmer for 30 minutes, or until syrupy. Add the slivered almonds and stir to combine. Continue cooking for another 30 minutes, adding the lemon juice, rosewater, and bloomed saffron in the last 5 minutes. If you're using pistachios, strain them and reserve. Discard the rosewater. Remove the pot from the heat and let the carrots cool. Once cool, stir in the pistachios (if using).

Serve the jam with flatbread and generous slabs of butter. The jam keeps in the refrigerator for 2 to 3 months.

ORANGE AND CARDAMOM FRENCH TOAST VEG

This might come as a surprise, but French toast is a huge piece of the *Maman and Me* story. When I was five years old, Maman signed us up for a mommy-and-me cooking class at our local community center. Together, we learned how to make simple dishes that were considered American classics. One of those dishes was French toast, which I took a strong liking to. In the years following the cooking class, Maman and I made French toast every single Sunday. French toast will always transport me back to those mommy-and-me moments, and now I'm sharing our twist on this classic breakfast.

Serves 4

——

1 cup (240 ml) heavy cream
   or whole milk

4 large eggs

2 Tbsp brown sugar

1 Tbsp grated orange zest

½ tsp vanilla extract

½ tsp ground cardamom

Fine salt

1 loaf brioche or challah, cut
   ¾ in (2 cm) thick slices

Unsalted butter, for cooking

Maple syrup, for serving

Confectioners' sugar,
   for serving

Fresh berries, for serving
   (optional)

In a large bowl, whisk together the heavy cream, eggs, brown sugar, orange zest, vanilla, cardamom, and a pinch of salt until evenly combined. Pour the egg mixture into a baking dish and arrange the bread slices inside. Soak the bread, flipping once, for 2 minutes total.

Meanwhile, melt 1 Tbsp of butter in a large pan over medium heat until lightly foamy. Working in batches, add a few slices of the soaked bread and cook, flipping once, for 2 minutes on each side, or until evenly browned. Repeat to cook the remaining French toast, adding more butter to the pan as needed.

Placed the finished French toast on a warm serving platter and serve with maple syrup, confectioners' sugar, and berries (if using). Leftover French toast will keep in the refrigerator for up to 3 days and makes a delicious base for a Sweet Labneh Toast (page 31).

ROSY PANCAKES VEG

Growing up, we used a box mix to make pancakes, doctoring the powdered mixture with spices and different ingredients, which was like doing a science experiment each time. We found that rosewater pairs beautifully with maple syrup, tasting like the syrupy sweet baked goods at an Iranian bakery. You can easily make this recipe using store-bought pancake mix and adding in rosewater, but I'm providing a fully homemade version. If you stock your pantry with orange-blossom water, you could substitute that or even top your pancakes with simple syrup spiked with saffron. If you really want to lean into the rose flavor and have a decadent breakfast, serve the pancakes with Rosewater Whipped Cream (page 180).

Makes 10 pancakes

——

1½ cups (210 g) all-purpose flour

1 Tbsp granulated sugar

1 tsp baking powder

½ tsp baking soda

¼ tsp fine salt

1¼ cups (300 ml) whole milk (or plant-based milk)

1 large egg

¼ cup (60 ml) rosewater

2 Tbsp unsalted butter, melted, plus more for cooking

Maple syrup, for serving

In a large bowl, whisk together the flour, sugar, baking powder, baking soda, and salt until evenly combined.

In a medium bowl, whisk together the milk, egg, rosewater, and 2 Tbsp of melted butter until evenly combined.

In a large nonstick pan over medium heat, melt a little butter.

While the pan is heating, make a well in the bowl of dry ingredients and pour in the wet ingredients. Gently and slowly fold to just combine, leaving lumps in the batter.

Working in batches, ladle the pancake mixture into the warm pan, pouring about ¼ cup (60 ml) at a time for each pancake. Let the pancakes cook until you see bubbles forming on top, then flip and continue cooking for 1 to 2 more minutes, until lightly golden. Repeat to cook the remaining pancakes, adding more butter to the pan as needed.

Serve warm with maple syrup.

TURKEY PORRIDGE, TWO WAYS (HALIM)

When I think of halim, I think of congee, jok moo, harees, and all the incredible meaty porridges from around the world. While these delicious dishes each have their own unique flavors and ingredients, the through line between them is that they provide lasting sustenance. Halim can be found in shops all over Iran, where people line up for a steaming hot bowl before their workdays, especially in the winter. A slowly simmered and stewed porridge that you can eat sweet *or* savory (plot twist!), halim makes the perfect start to your day. We prefer ours sweet, but I recommend playing around with different flavor combinations and toppings—a runny egg, chili crisp, and wilted greens can take savory halim to the next level. Pelted or pearled wheat can be found online or at Southwest Asian grocers, and if you can't find turkey legs, turkey breasts or even lamb shoulder would work as a substitute.

Serves 4 to 6

——

3 cups (570 g) pelted or
   pearled wheat, washed
   thoroughly
1 lb (455 g) skin-on, bone-in
   turkey legs or breasts
1 yellow onion, top and
   bottom removed
1 tsp fine salt
3 Tbsp vegetable oil

SWEET HALIM
Melted unsalted butter,
   for serving
Granulated sugar, for serving
Ground cinnamon,
   for serving
Heavy cream, for serving
   (optional)

SAVORY HALIM
Flaky sea salt, for serving

In a large pot, cover the pelted or pearled wheat, turkey, and onion with water until the turkey is just covered. Add the salt, turn the heat to high, and bring to a boil. Once boiling, skim any dark foam off the top and add the oil to prevent overflowing. Turn the heat to low and cook until the turkey is completely cooked through and tender, about 1 hour. Remove the onion and the turkey, including the skin, from the pot. Remove and discard the turkey skin, cartilage, and bones, as well as the onion. Using two forks, shred the turkey and set aside.

With an immersion blender, blend the wheat in the pan until creamy and uniform. Return the shredded turkey to the pot and stir to incorporate. If the mixture is too thick (not porridge-like), add hot water, ½ cup (120 ml) at a time, stirring constantly, until you get the desired consistency. Let the halim continue cooking over low heat, stirring occasionally, until creamy and thickened and pulling away from the pan around the edges, about 30 minutes.

When ready to serve, pour the halim into serving bowls and add the sweet or savory toppings. Halim will keep in the refrigerator for up to 5 days.

Mazzeh: Snacks & Sides

Citrus-Roasted Almonds
VGN · GF — 46

Stuffed Dates, Two Ways
VGN · GF — 49

Olive, Pomegranate, and Walnut Tapenade (Zeytoon Parvardeh)
VGN · GF — 50

Cooling Cucumber Yogurt (Mast-o Khiar)
VEG · GF — 53

Potato Chips and Greek Yogurt Dip (Chips-o Mast)
VEG — 54

Honey-Drizzled Feta in Phyllo Dough
VEG — 57

Spring Herb Frittatas (Kuku Sabzi)
VEG — 58

Green Bean Frittata (Kuku Loobia Sabz)
VEG · GF — 61

Potato Pancakes (Kuku Sibzamini)
VEG — 62

Garlicky Eggplant Dip (Kashk Bademjoon)
VEG · GF — 65

Wonton Wrapper Sambusas with Tamarind Dipping Sauce (Sambuseh)
VEG — 67

Vinegary Chopped Pickles (Torshi Liteh)
VGN · GF — 70

Salt Pickles (Shoor)
VGN · GF — 73

CITRUS-ROASTED ALMONDS VGN · GF

One of the best gifts to receive when someone returns from Iran (other than saffron) is ajil: mixed nuts with delicious seasonings. I've always had a hard time finding the same style nuts in the United States, until I learned that the secret ingredient is citrus! These almonds are an attempt to replicate the salty, sour snack I long for.

Makes 2 cups (280 g)

———

1 large lemon, zested and juiced

1 tsp fine salt

2 cups (280 g) raw, unsalted almonds

Preheat the oven to 350°F (180°C).

In a small bowl, whisk together the lemon juice, lemon zest, and salt.

Spread the almonds on a baking sheet and bake, shaking the baking sheet every 5 minutes, for 15 to 20 minutes. Once you can smell the almonds, turn off the oven; you want the nuts fragrant but not browned. Pour the lemon salt mixture over the almonds, return them to the oven, and close the oven door. Let the almonds absorb the lemon juice and dry out from the residual heat of the oven for an additional 10 to 20 minutes, checking occasionally to make sure the nuts don't burn.

Roasted almonds will keep in an airtight container at room temperature for up to 1 month.

STUFFED DATES, TWO WAYS VGN · GF

Dates are a powerhouse snack. At their best, they taste like nature's candy (and now I officially sound like my grandma, Maman Bozorg). There are loads of ways to stuff dates and I'm sharing two of my favorites. These both lean sweet, but you could forego the rosewater and substitute a salty cheese to pair with walnuts for something more savory.

Serves 4, as an appetizer

———

DATES STUFFED WITH PEANUT BUTTER

12 large Medjool dates

¼ cup (65 g) creamy peanut butter

Cinnamon, for topping (optional)

Pomegranate seeds, for topping (optional)

WARM DATES STUFFED WITH ROSEWATER AND WALNUTS

12 large Medjool dates

¼ cup (60 ml) rosewater, for dipping

12 walnut halves (if your dates are large enough, whole walnuts will work!)

To make the dates stuffed with peanut butter:
Using a small, sharp knife, make a small lengthwise incision in each date and remove the pit. Arrange the dates, cut-side up, on a plate or serving dish, and carefully spoon a small amount of peanut butter (about 1 tsp) into each one. If desired, you can bake the dates in a 200°F (95°C) oven for about 5 minutes, or until the peanut butter melts and the dates are warmed through. Top the stuffed dates with a sprinkle of cinnamon or pomegranate seeds, if desired. Serve immediately.

To make the warm dates stuffed with rosewater and walnuts:
Preheat the oven to 350°F (180°C). Using a small sharp knife, make a small lengthwise incision in each date and remove the pit. Pour the rosewater into a small bowl. Dip the dates in the rosewater, then place them, cut-side up, on a baking sheet. Place a walnut half inside each date. Bake for 10 minutes, or until the dates are warmed through. Serve immediately.

Store any remaining stuffed dates in the refrigerator for up to a week or in the freezer for up to 2 months.

OLIVE, POMEGRANATE, AND WALNUT TAPENADE (ZEYTOON PARVARDEH) VGN · GF

This briny, tart, and crunchy dip from northern Iran is an ideal treat at any gathering. We love to spread it on toasts and sandwiches and bring it to dinner parties, as it goes just as nicely with martinis as it does with wine. It's also easy to make and just needs some time to marinate and set in the refrigerator. Plus, it's the kind of recipe that you can make while friends are over or with little ones around, especially if you have a mortar and pestle, allowing people to take turns mashing and grinding the tapenade together.

Serves 4, as an appetizer

⸺

1 cup (140 g) unsalted
    walnuts, finely chopped
½ cup (20 g) finely chopped
    fresh mint
2 garlic cloves, minced
½ cup (120 ml) pomegranate
    molasses
3 Tbsp extra-virgin olive oil
1 tsp ground Angelica powder
    (optional)
Two 6 oz (170 g) cans
    pitted green olives,
    coarsely chopped
Fine salt and freshly ground
    black pepper
Pomegranate seeds, for
    serving (optional)

In a large bowl or using a large mortar and pestle, stir and grind the walnuts, mint, and garlic together. Whisk in the pomegranate molasses, oil, and Angelica powder (if using) until combined. Add the olives and stir to combine. Cover the bowl with plastic wrap, or place the tapenade in a airtight container, and set in the refrigerator to marinate. This dip is best served after sitting in the refrigerator overnight (and continues to get better with time), but it can be enjoyed a few hours afterward. Taste before serving and top with salt and pepper as needed, along with pomegranate seeds. The tapenade will keep in an airtight container in the refrigerator for up to 1 week.

COOLING CUCUMBER YOGURT (MAST-O KHIAR) VEG · GF

Mast-o khiar is a side that's the perfect match for hearty Iranian dishes and a great treat in the warmer months. We typically eat it with our pilafs, like Loobia Polo (page 129), or dunk bread in it as a snack. The star here is dried mint—you can add any additional dried herbs you have on hand, but mint on its own will always be delicious.

Serves 5

———

4 Persian cucumbers, peeled and grated

2 cups (480 g) Greek yogurt

1 tsp dried mint

Fine salt and freshly ground black pepper

Dried roses or rose petals, lightly crushed, for garnish (optional)

Using a cheesecloth or clean kitchen towel, squeeze the grated cucumbers over the sink to remove excess water. Put the yogurt in a medium serving bowl, add the grated cucumber, and stir until evenly combined. Add the dried mint and any other herbs you might be using and stir until fully incorporated. Taste the mixture before seasoning with salt and black pepper.

Serve, sprinkled with dried roses or rose petals if you have them— they make for a beautiful, traditional garnish. Mast-o khiar will keep in an airtight container in the refrigerator for up to 5 days.

POTATO CHIPS AND GREEK YOGURT DIP (CHIPS-O MAST) VEG

This is my favorite Iranian snack of all time. It takes me back to coming home after school and having some chips and dip to tide me over until dinner. The combination of salty potato chips and creamy, thick yogurt is divine. Growing up, we would use any brand of potato chips we could find, but while in college I discovered that Cheddar & Sour Cream Ruffles make an incredible pairing for this dip. My older sister's trick is to take the dregs at the bottom of the chip bag and pour them straight into the dip and eat it with a spoon—we call this "soup."

Serves 2

——

1 cup (240 g) Greek yogurt

¼ cup (60 g) mayonnaise

1 tsp Italian seasoning (or dried oregano or another dried herb)

¼ tsp garlic powder

¼ tsp onion powder

Fine salt and freshly ground black pepper

Potato chips, for serving

Put the yogurt in a small serving bowl. Stir in the mayonnaise until the mixture is smooth and free of lumps. Stir in whatever dried herbs you're using, as well as the garlic powder and onion powder. Using a chip as a dipper, taste the dip before seasoning it with salt and pepper—chips are quite salty, so you don't want to overdo it. Serve with chips alongside. The dip will keep in an airtight container in the refrigerator for 2 days.

To make soup, either pour the crumbs from the bottom of the chip bag directly into your dip and stir to combine or crush whole chips before pouring them into the dip.

HONEY-DRIZZLED FETA IN PHYLLO DOUGH VEG

Iranian cuisine isn't heavy on cheese, but the one cheese we consistently enjoy is feta. We eat this salty, briny cheese for breakfast and lunch, throw it in our salads, and smush it into a loqme with our favorite herbs. As Maman got acquainted with Western-style entertaining, she saw (and enjoyed) a lot of baked Brie. She loved the combination of creamy cheese, sweet jam, and puff pastry, and one day, inspiration struck to replicate this dish with our treasured feta. We substitute honey for the jam and phyllo dough for the puff pastry, and the result is crunchy, flaky, sweet, and salty all at once.

Serves 4

———

One 8 oz (230 g) block feta cheese, drained and patted dry

3 sheets frozen phyllo dough, thawed

Extra-virgin olive oil, for brushing

Honey, for drizzling

Fresh thyme, for garnish (optional)

Set a rack in the middle of the oven and preheat the oven to 350°F (180°C).

Cut the feta into twelve 1 in (2.5 cm) cubes and set aside.

Place one sheet of phyllo dough on a baking sheet and brush lightly with the oil. Place the second sheet of phyllo directly on top and brush with the oil. Repeat the process once more with the third sheet of phyllo and the oil. Spread the feta cubes evenly on top of the layered sheets of phyllo, then cut the phyllo lengthwise and widthwise in between the feta, so there are squares of phyllo under each feta cube. Wrap the phyllo squares around the feta cubes and put the pastry packets in a muffin tin. Bake on the middle rack for 15 to 20 minutes, or until lightly golden.

Drizzle with honey and sprinkle with fresh thyme, if desired. Serve warm.

SPRING HERB FRITTATAS (KUKU SABZI) VEG

Kuku is the name for egg-based frittatas mixed with vegetables and other ingredients. Kuku sabzi is full of herbs and perfect for brunch, snack time, or as a dinner side. After Maman made kuku sabzi for the thousandth time for an Iranian New Year party, she had an epiphany. Rather than making it in a skillet, she could use cupcake tins so everyone could have their own portion with an ideal ratio of crisp edges to soft middle. We experimented with different ingredient ratios and cooking times to perfect it, and voilà. We're sharing the technique for small kuku cakes baked in a muffin tin in the oven, as well as how to make one larger kuku on the stovetop.

**Makes 1 large kuku or
12 individual kuku cakes**

———

6 large eggs

1 Tbsp all-purpose flour

1 tsp baking powder

1 tsp ground turmeric

1 tsp fine salt

**½ tsp freshly ground
  black pepper**

**2 cups (80 g) chopped fresh
  flat-leaf parsley**

**2 cups (80 g) chopped
  fresh cilantro**

**1 cup (40 g) finely chopped
  fresh dill**

**½ cup (24 g) finely chopped
  fresh chives**

**½ cup (24 g) finely chopped
  green onions**

4 garlic cloves, grated

**1 heaping Tbsp finely
  chopped walnuts (optional)**

**1 heaping Tbsp barberries
  (optional)**

⅓ cup (80 ml) vegetable oil

Cooking spray

In a large bowl, beat the eggs until uniform in color. Whisk in the flour, baking powder, turmeric, salt, and pepper. Stir in the parsley, cilantro, dill, chives, green onions, garlic, walnuts (if using), and barberries (if using). The kuku mixture should just barely bind together: The less eggy the batter, the more green the end result will be.

If you'd like to make one large kuku on the stove, warm the oil in a large frying pan over medium heat until glistening. Pour in the egg and herb mixture and let cook for 10 to 15 minutes, checking the bottom after 10 minutes to see if it's browned. Using a wooden spatula, divide the kuku into fourths or sixths, and flip the pieces over. Cook uncovered for another 10 to 15 minutes, or until lightly browned on both sides. Place the kuku pieces on a platter lined with paper towels to soak up any excess oil. Flip the pieces and leave for a few more minutes.

If you want to make individual kuku cakes, set a rack in the middle of the oven and preheat the oven to 350°F (180°C). Spray a muffin tin generously with cooking spray.

Whisk the oil into the egg and herb mixture to combine. Spoon the kuku mixture into the muffin tin, filling each cup about two-thirds full. Bake for 25 to 30 minutes, or until the kuku cakes are light brown and a cake tester inserted in the middle of a kuku cake comes out clean.

Kuku is delicious warm or cold and will keep in the refrigerator for up to 1 week. It can also be frozen for up to 3 months and reheated in the oven.

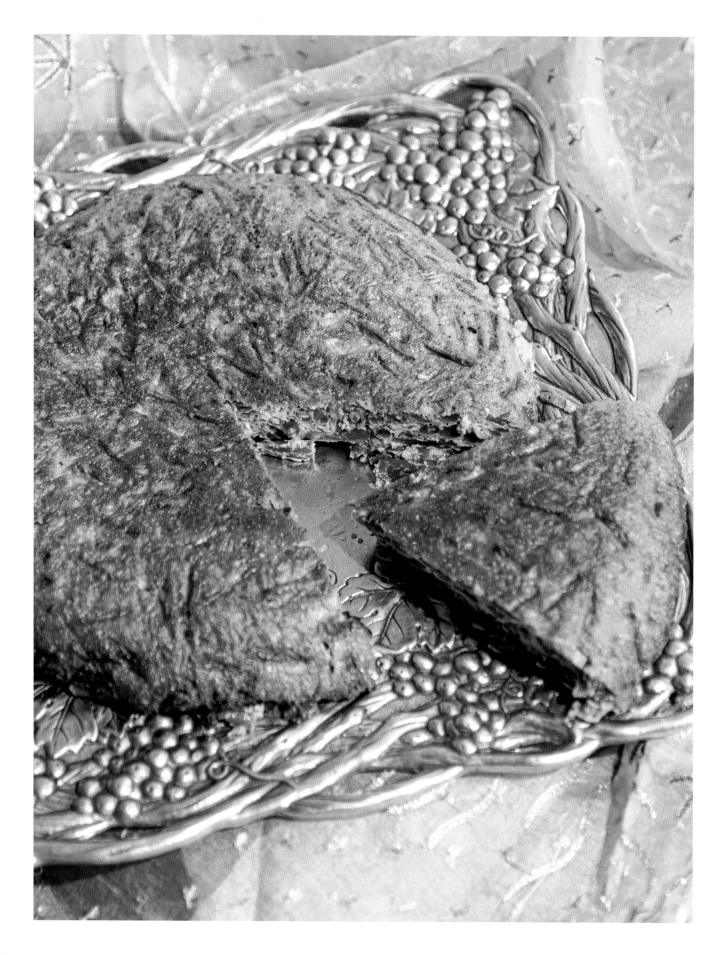

GREEN BEAN FRITTATA (KUKU LOOBIA SABZ) VEG · GF

Kuku sabzi (page 58) might be the most famous Iranian kuku, but we have a few lesser-known frittatas that are just as easy to make—and just as tasty! Kukus were go-to dishes for my mom as a college student living on her own and they have become easy favorites for me. This recipe explains how to make one large kuku that can be cut into pieces, but if you're brave, you can try keeping the frittata intact by flipping it onto a plate and returning it to the pan, when you're ready to turn it over. Kuku loobia sabz can also be made into individual fritters, following the method from the next recipe, for Potato Pancakes (Kuku Sibzamini, on page 62).

Makes 1 large kuku

——

1 lb (455 g) fresh green beans, trimmed and cut into 1 in (2.5 cm) pieces
5 large eggs
½ tsp fine salt
¼ tsp freshly ground black pepper
1 tsp ground turmeric
1 Tbsp all-purpose flour
⅓ cup (80 ml) vegetable oil

Fill a medium pot with water, add a dash of salt, and bring to a boil. Fill a large bowl with ice water. Add the green beans to the boiling water and cook for 3 to 5 minutes, or until bright green and warmed through. Drain the green beans and immediately plunge into the ice water to stop the cooking and preserve the color. Drain the green beans again, then dry with paper towels or a kitchen towel.

In a large bowl, beat the eggs with the salt, pepper, and turmeric. Stir in the green beans, followed by the flour.

Heat the oil in a medium frying pan over medium heat until glistening. Add the kuku mixture and let cook for 5 to 10 minutes, or until the bottom is set. Using a wooden spatula, cut the kuku into fourths and flip the pieces over. Cover and let cook for another 5 to 7 minutes, or until lightly golden on both sides. Place the kuku pieces on a platter lined with paper towels to soak up any excess oil. Flip the pieces and leave for a few more minutes.

Kuku is delicious warm or cold and will keep in the refrigerator for up to 1 week. It can also be frozen for up to 3 months and reheated in the oven.

POTATO PANCAKES (KUKU SIBZAMINI) VEG

These potato pancakes are similar to latkes and hash browns. The addition of turmeric gives them a gorgeous golden color and a burst of delicious flavor. In my family, we make these for breakfast, lunch, and dinner—truly whenever we're craving them. They are perfect for dipping in ketchup or sour cream, or on their own topped with flaky sea salt.

Serves 4, as a side

———

2 large russet potatoes, peeled and grated

1 medium yellow onion, grated

2 garlic cloves, minced

2 large eggs

1 Tbsp all-purpose flour

1 tsp ground turmeric

1 tsp fine salt

¼ tsp freshly ground black pepper

1 cup (240 ml) vegetable oil

Ketchup, for serving

Using a cheesecloth or kitchen towel, squeeze the grated potatoes over the sink several times to remove excess water. Put the potatoes in a medium bowl, along with the onion, garlic, eggs, flour, turmeric, salt, and pepper. Stir to combine using a whisk or a wooden spoon.

Heat the oil in a large frying pan or pot over medium heat. To check if the oil is warm enough, place the end of a spatula into the oil—if the oil bubbles around it, it's ready. Working in batches, use an ice cream scoop or a ladle to gently drop a few scoops of the potato mixture into the hot oil. Cook for about 1 minute, then use a spatula to gently flatten the pancakes. Cook for 2 to 3 more minutes, or until the bottoms are golden, then flip the pancakes and cook on the other side for an additional 2 minutes, or until golden and crisp all over. Place the pancakes on a serving platter lined with paper towels to soak up any excess oil. Continue cooking more pancakes, adjusting the heat as needed.

Serve warm with ketchup. The potato pancakes will keep in the refrigerator for up to 3 days.

GARLICKY EGGPLANT DIP (KASHK BADEMJOON) VEG · GF

Kashk bademjoon tastes like baba ghanoush's cool and elusive, slightly mysterious older sibling. The star ingredient here is kashk (yogurt whey), a thick, salty Iranian dairy product that gives the dip an assertive umami flavor that's not unlike Parmesan. You can find kashk at most Southwest Asian grocers, in the refrigerated area with other dairy products, or substitute it with sour cream or Greek yogurt. This spread is topped with saffron, blackened mint, caramelized onions, and more kashk for even more flavor—you can always prepare the toppings ahead of time to speed up the cooking process. If you want crunch and textural contrast, you can add finely chopped walnuts.

Serves 6, as an appetizer

———

Fine salt

4 large eggplants, peeled
    and cut into 1 in (2.5 cm)
    thick rounds

3 Tbsp vegetable oil, plus
    ½ cup (120 ml)

1 medium yellow onion,
    chopped

Black pepper

2 tsp ground turmeric

1 tsp curry powder

10 garlic cloves, thinly sliced

3 Tbsp dried mint

½ cup (110 g) liquid kashk
    (or sour cream or Greek
    yogurt), plus more for
    serving

½ cup (120 ml) boiling water

Red pepper flakes (optional)

½ cup (60 g) finely chopped
    walnuts, plus more
    for serving (optional)

Pinch of saffron threads
    (optional)

Flatbread, naan, or crackers,
    for serving

Generously salt the eggplant on both sides and leave it in a strainer, so it can release some moisture, for at least 30 minutes or up to 1 hour. While the eggplant drains, prepare your toppings.

Heat 3 Tbsp (45 ml) of the oil in a medium sauté pan over medium-high heat. Add the onion and cook, stirring occasionally, for 8 to 10 minutes, or until soft and lightly golden (do not caramelize). Sprinkle with a pinch of salt and pepper, then add the turmeric and curry powder. Remove the pan from the heat, then use a slotted spoon to transfer the onions to a plate and set aside. Do not discard the oil.

Heat the pan with the oil over medium heat. Add the garlic and cook for 1 to 2 minutes, or until lightly golden. Remove the pan from the heat, then use the slotted spoon to transfer the garlic to a plate and set aside. Do not discard the oil.

Heat the pan with the oil over medium heat. Add the dried mint and stir quickly, so it absorbs the oil, then immediately remove the pan from the heat (it gets bitter quickly!).

Pat the eggplant slices dry with a paper towel.

Heat the remaining ½ cup (120 ml) of oil in a frying pan over medium heat. Working in batches, add the eggplant and fry on both sides for 3 to 4 minutes per side, or until light golden. Transfer the eggplant to a platter lined with paper towels (or a strainer) to drain any excess oil. Do not discard the oil.

continues →

GARLICKY EGGPLANT DIP (KASHK BADEMJOON)

In a small bowl, dilute the kashk with the boiling water and mix until smooth. If you're using sour cream or yogurt, add the boiling water in the next step.

Heat the frying pan with the oil over low heat. Add a third of the cooked onions, garlic, and mint, and all the eggplant. With a fork or potato masher, mash the eggplant. Sprinkle with a pinch of red pepper flakes, if using. Add the diluted kashk (or if you're using sour cream or yogurt, just add the boiling water for now). Cook, stirring occasionally, for 20 minutes, or until the water has completely evaporated and the mixture has a thick, porridge-like consistency.

If you're using sour cream or yogurt, add it to the eggplant mixture and let it boil for 5 minutes. Stir in the walnuts (if using) and remove from the heat.

Pour the eggplant mixture into a large serving dish. Drizzle the kashk all over and top with the remaining onion, garlic, and mint, along with more walnuts (if using), in whichever way looks and feels right to you: My mom makes checkerboard patterns and flowers with her kashk toppings; I throw them all over, Jackson Pollock–style. If you have saffron threads, you can bloom a pinch of them in 1 Tbsp of hot water and spoon the golden liquid on top.

Serve kashk bademjoon with flatbread, naan, or crackers. It is great warm or at room temperature, so try it both ways and discover your favorite! It will keep in the refrigerator for up to 5 days.

WONTON WRAPPER SAMBUSAS WITH TAMARIND DIPPING SAUCE (SAMBUSEH) VEG

I'm not entirely sure where Maman learned the trick of using wonton wrappers to make sambusas, but I'm guessing it was on one of her many loud, gossip-filled, belly-laughing phone calls with aunties and friends. Truly, the farther these people are geographically, the louder their voices get. I digress. Thanks to wonton wrappers, which can be found in the refrigerated or frozen aisles of most grocery stores, this recipe comes together quickly and beautifully. For a vegetarian alternative, you can substitute the ground beef for 1½ cups (180 g) of frozen peas and use two potatoes in the filling instead of one. The sweet, sour, and spicy dipping sauce features tamarind pulp, often found in dark brown bricks in South Asian and Latino grocers.

**Makes about
25 sambusas**

——

FILLING

1 large russet potato,
    unpeeled
1 Tbsp vegetable oil,
    plus more for frying
1 lb (455 g) ground beef
1 large yellow onion, grated
    or finely chopped
4 garlic cloves, minced
2 green onions, thinly sliced
¼ cup (10 g) finely chopped
    fresh cilantro
2 Tbsp finely chopped fresh
    flat-leaf parsley
1 Tbsp tomato paste
1 Tbsp fresh lemon juice
1 tsp ground turmeric
1 tsp fine salt
1 tsp pepper
Red pepper flakes (optional)

SAMBUSAS

1 Tbsp all-purpose flour
One 16 oz (455 g) package
    wonton wrappers
About ½ cup (120 ml)
    vegetable oil, for frying

TAMARIND DIPPING SAUCE

½ cup (100 g) tamarind paste,
    plus more as needed
A few dashes of hot sauce
    (we love Sriracha)
3 Tbsp any combination of
    chopped fresh flat-leaf parsley,
    cilantro, or green onions

To make the filling:

In a medium saucepan, cover the potato with cold water. Cover and bring to a boil over high heat. Continue boiling for 10 to 15 minutes, periodically checking to see if the potato is tender.

Meanwhile, heat the oil in a large sauté pan over medium heat. Add the ground beef and cook, stirring occasionally and breaking up any chunks, for about 5 minutes, or until evenly browned. Add the onion, garlic, green onions, cilantro, parsley, tomato paste, lemon juice, turmeric, salt, pepper, and red pepper flakes (if using) and stir to combine. Cover and cook for 5 more minutes.

Once the potato is cooked and cool enough to handle, peel off the skin (it should slide off easily). Chop the potato into small, bite-size pieces, then add it to the ground beef mixture and stir to combine.

continues →

WONTON WRAPPER SAMBUSAS

To assemble the sambusas (this is the fun part):
In a small bowl, stir the flour into 2 Tbsp of water to make a paste—this is your glue.

Working with one wonton wrapper at a time, place a spoonful of the ground beef mixture in the center of a wonton square. Dip your fingers into the flour glue and rub it along the edges of the wonton wrapper. Grab one corner of the wrapper and fold it over diagonally to create a triangle. Put gentle pressure on the filling to push out any air, then pinch the edges to seal them. Repeat with the remaining wonton wrappers and filling. The uncooked sambusas will keep beautifully in the freezer for up to 2 months. They're great to have on hand when you have people over or whenever you want a late-night sambusa.

To make the dipping sauce:
In a small saucepan, bring 1 cup (240 ml) of water to a boil over high heat. Add the tamarind paste and continue boiling, stirring occasionally, for 5 to 7 minutes. If the mixture is too thick, add more boiling or hot water and stir. If the mixture is too thin or needs more flavor, add more tamarind paste. When you have a saucy consistency (think ketchup), remove the mixture from the heat. Stir in the hot sauce and let cool.

When the sauce is lukewarm, stir in the chopped herbs. We find it easy to heap this sauce all over the sambusas, so you might not have any left over…but if you do (lucky you!), it will keep in the refrigerator for up to 3 days.

To fry the sambusas:
Fill a frying pan with 1 in (2.5 cm) of the oil and put over medium heat. Let the oil warm up for 2 minutes before frying the sambusas. Working in batches, carefully add a few sambusas to the hot oil and fry for 2 to 3 minutes, or until the edges are lightly golden. Using tongs, flip the sambusas over and continue cooking for 2 to 3 more minutes, or until uniformly golden. Immediately transfer the sambusas to a platter lined with paper towels and let cool slightly. Repeat to fry the remaining sambusas, adjusting the heat as needed.

Serve the sambusas warm with the dipping sauce. They will keep in an airtight container in the refrigerator for several days and are best reheated in the oven.

VINEGARY CHOPPED PICKLES (TORSHI LITEH) VGN · GF

There are two genres of pickles in Iranian cuisine: vinegar-based torshi (sour) and salt-based shoor (salty, page 73). This pickle is more like a relish, packed with finely chopped veggies, smashed eggplant, and herbs. It's great to make with any combination of fresh vegetables; if you don't feel like chopping, using a food processor will make it easier. Angelica powder, which you can find in a Southwest Asian grocer or online, is the special ingredient that gives these pickles some earthiness. You can serve this pickle as a topping or condiment with any main dish.

Makes two 16 oz (455 g) jars

———

5 medium eggplants, peeled and cut into small chunks

2 cups (480 ml) distilled white vinegar

4 Tbsp fine salt

1 head cauliflower, cut into small florets

1 lb (455 g) carrots, grated

2 heads garlic, cloves separated, peeled, and minced

1 jalapeño, seeded and finely chopped

⅓ cup (15 g) finely chopped fresh flat-leaf parsley

⅓ cup (15 g) finely chopped fresh mint

⅓ cup (15 g) finely chopped fresh basil

⅓ cup (15 g) finely chopped fresh tarragon (optional)

1 Tbsp ground Angelica powder

1 tsp whole caraway seeds

1 Tbsp whole black peppercorns

1 Tbsp ground turmeric

1 cup (240 ml) red wine vinegar

In a large pot, cover the eggplant with water. Add 1 cup (240 ml) of the distilled white vinegar and 2 Tbsp of the salt and bring to a boil over high heat. Continue boiling for 5 minutes, then drain the eggplant, discarding the water. Leave the eggplant in the strainer and set a plate with a cast-iron skillet or anything heavy on top to compress the eggplant and squeeze out any excess moisture. Let drain for at least 2 hours or overnight.

In a large bowl, combine the eggplant with the cauliflower, carrots, garlic, jalapeño, parsley, mint, basil, tarragon, Angelica powder, caraway seeds, peppercorns, and turmeric and mix to fully combine. Fill sterilized glass jars about two-thirds full with the vegetable mixture.

Combine the remaining 1 cup (240 ml) of distilled white vinegar with the red wine vinegar, then pour into the jars until the vegetables are covered; reserve the leftover vinegar mixture. Leave the jars uncovered at room temperature overnight.

The following morning, add more of the remaining vinegar mixture to fill the jars almost to the top. Use plastic wrap to cover the inside of the lids so they don't touch the vinegar. Seal the jars and store them in the refrigerator. The pickles will be ready in 2 weeks but will keep in the refrigerator for up to 1 month.

SALT PICKLES (SHOOR) VGN · GF

These pickles taste more like the conventional pickles you're used to and can be made with a variety of vegetables. We love finding tiny cucumbers and keeping them whole here, but you can also slice up standard Persian cucumbers instead. Chickpeas are the most interesting ingredient in the recipe and allegedly help kick-start the fermentation and create better flavor. I don't have science to back this up—just Maman's intuition!

Makes two 16 oz (455 g) jars

—

½ head cauliflower, chopped
    into florets

1 lb (455 g) carrots,
    cut into 1 in (2.5 cm)
    thick rounds

3 jalapeños, seeded and
    cut into ¼ in (6 mm)
    thick rounds

5 baby cucumbers

1 head garlic, cloves
    separated and peeled

1 handful fresh dill, separated
    into individual stems

1 handful dried chickpeas

2 Tbsp fine salt

2 cups (480 ml) white vinegar

In a large bowl, combine the cauliflower, carrots, jalapeños, cucumbers, garlic, and dill. Pour into sterilized jars, adding a few dried chickpeas to each jar.

Fill a medium pot with 4 cups (960 ml) of water and bring to a boil over medium heat. Add the salt and once it's dissolved, turn off the heat. Let the saltwater cool to room temperature, then use a ladle to pour it into the jars, leaving a 1 in (2.5 cm) gap at the top. Reserve any remaining saltwater in a sealed container. Pour the white vinegar into the jars to fill the 1 in (2.5 cm) gap. Leave the jars uncovered at room temperature for 24 hours.

The following day, if there is extra space at the top of the jars, add more of the reserved saltwater. Seal the jars and store them in the refrigerator. The pickles will be ready in 7 to 10 days but will keep in the refrigerator for up to 1 month.

Salads & Soups

Everyday Cucumber and Tomato Salad (Salad Shirazi)
VGN · GF — 77

Beet and Labneh Salad (Borani-e Labu)
VEG · GF — 78

Squash Salad with Pomegranate Molasses Dressing
VGN · GF — 81

The Trifecta: Chicken, Potato, and Egg Salad (Salad Olivieh)
GF — 82

Chilled Yogurt and Herb Soup (Ab Doogh Khiar)
VEG — 85

Tomato and Egg Drop Soup (Eshkane)
VEG · GF — 86

Spiced Red Lentil Soup (Dal Adasi)
VGN · GF — 89

Creamy Leek and Potato Soup with Turmeric and Carrots
VEG · GF — 90

Three Bean and Noodle Soup (Ash-e Reshteh)
VEG — 93

Creamy Chicken, Barley, and Vegetable Soup (Soup-e Jo)
96

Hearty Lamb, Bean, and Potato Soup (Abgoosht)
GF — 97

EVERYDAY CUCUMBER AND TOMATO SALAD (SALAD SHIRAZI) VGN · GF

Salad Shirazi originated in Shiraz and is a ubiquitous staple at nearly every meal (except for our beloved chai and cookies) across Iranian tables. It's similar to pico de gallo or kachumber, just with extra zing from plenty of lime juice. As much a salad as it is a condiment, salad Shirazi goes beautifully with the savory stews in this book. The best part is the leftover vinaigrette at the bottom of the bowl—Maman and I fight over who gets to drink it. Sumac is a great addition for more zest and citrus flavor and is available at Southwest Asian grocers.

Serves 4, as a side

———

4 Persian cucumbers

½ red onion, cut into ¼ in (6 mm) pieces

3 medium Roma tomatoes, diced

1 Tbsp dried mint (or 2 tsp finely chopped fresh mint)

3 Tbsp fresh lime juice, plus more as needed

3 Tbsp extra-virgin olive oil

Fine salt and freshly ground black pepper

Sumac (optional)

Trim the ends of the cucumbers, then use a vegetable peeler to remove alternating strips of the peel if you're feeling fancy! Cut the cucumbers lengthwise in half, then cut each half lengthwise again to get 4 quarters. Cut each quarter crosswise into ¼ in (6 mm) triangular pieces and put in a medium bowl, along with the red onion.

If the tomatoes are particularly juicy, put them in a colander for a few minutes to release some liquid, then add them to the cucumber and red onion mixture. Add the dried mint (or fresh mint, if using) and gently stir to combine.

In a small bowl, whisk together the lime juice, olive oil, generous pinches of salt and pepper, and a sprinkle of sumac (if using) for extra brightness! Taste the vinaigrette: It should be sour enough to make your mouth pucker. Add more lime juice or salt as needed.

If you want the salad on the crunchier side, add the dressing immediately before serving, and season with additional salt, pepper, and sumac (if using). If you want the salad on the juicier side, stir in the dressing, season, and let the salad sit in the refrigerator for 30 minutes to 1 hour before serving. Leftovers will keep in the refrigerator for up to 2 days.

BEET AND LABNEH SALAD (BORANI-E LABU) VEG · GF

Borani-e labu is traditionally a yogurt-based dip, similar to Mast-o Khiar (page 53), that takes on a gorgeous pink hue thanks to the beets. Maman and I prefer this deconstructed version that is more of a salad than a dip. It's incredibly simple and makes a stunning addition to any meal or mezze spread. The earthiness of the beets is the perfect match for creamy labneh, with a touch of mint for some cooling freshness.

Serves 2

---

8 oz (230 g) beets (about 4
    medium beets), peeled
½ cup (120 g) labneh
1 Tbsp finely chopped fresh
    mint, plus more to taste
Extra-virgin olive oil,
    for drizzling
Flaky salt and freshly
    ground black pepper

Preheat the oven to 400°F (200°C).

Wrap the beets loosely in aluminum foil, arrange on a baking sheet, and bake for 1 hour. Check the beets with a fork every 20 minutes— if any of the beets are looking dry, you can pour 1 Tbsp of water on top. The beets are done when they're fork-tender. Allow them to cool completely before cutting into rounds.

Spoon dollops of labneh across a large plate or serving platter, making ridges and waves with the back of the spoon. Arrange the beet slices on top of the labneh, then scatter fresh mint on top, drizzle with olive oil, and season with salt and pepper.

Serve immediately.

SQUASH SALAD WITH POMEGRANATE MOLASSES DRESSING VGN · GF

This salad is one of my standbys in the fall and anytime I have people over. It's the sort of salad that excites guests and just so happens to be vegan. Pomegranate seeds and pomegranate molasses lend both sweetness and tartness and are fabulous additions to nearly any salad—pomegranate seeds are easily found in the prepared food section of grocery stores, while pomegranate molasses can be found in Southwest Asian grocers and online. Goat cheese or feta would be a lovely add-in for some tang and creaminess!

Serves 2, as a main, or 4, as a side

———

SALAD

3 Tbsp extra-virgin olive oil

1 Tbsp maple syrup

1 tsp fine salt

½ tsp freshly ground black pepper, plus more as needed

1 medium butternut squash, peeled and cut into ½ in (13 mm) chunks

10 oz (280 g) spring mix or any tender fresh greens

½ cup (25 g) shredded carrot (about 1 medium carrot)

½ cup (87 g) pomegranate seeds

¼ cup (35 g) pumpkin seeds, toasted

Flaky salt

DRESSING

½ cup (120 ml) extra-virgin olive oil

3 Tbsp pomegranate molasses

1 Tbsp balsamic vinegar

1 Tbsp honey

Fine salt and freshly ground black pepper

Preheat the oven to 400°F (200°C).

To make the salad:

In a small bowl, whisk together the olive oil, maple syrup, fine salt, and pepper.

Spread the squash on a parchment paper–lined baking sheet, pour the maple mixture over the squash, and toss to evenly coat. Roast the squash, shaking the pan once or twice, for 20 minutes, or until lightly browned and fork-tender. Set aside to cool.

In a large salad bowl, combine the spring mix, carrot, pomegranate seeds, and pumpkin seeds.

To make the dressing:

In a small bowl, whisk together the oil, pomegranate molasses, vinegar, and honey until evenly combined. Taste the dressing and add salt and pepper as needed.

Add the cooled squash to the salad mixture, along with the dressing, and gently toss to combine. Season with flaky salt and freshly ground pepper and toss again.

Serve immediately.

THE TRIFECTA: CHICKEN, POTATO, AND EGG SALAD (SALAD OLIVIEH) GF

American cuisine is full of interesting mayonnaise-based salads, which we're still learning about decades into living here. There's only one similar Iranian dish, which combines the best parts of egg salad, chicken salad, and potato salad all in one, with veggies and pickles for crunch. You can find Iranian pickles in most Southwest Asian grocers or online. Zarrin's Pickled Midget Cucumbers are our go-to, but any cornichons will work!

Serves 6

——

2 large russet potatoes,
    peeled
6 large eggs
1 cup (140 g) frozen pea
    and carrot mix
1 large (or 2 small) chicken
    breasts
1 small white onion, peeled
2 garlic cloves
1 tsp fine salt
½ tsp black pepper
One 13½ fl oz (400 ml)
    jar cornichons or Iranian
    pickles, drained, finely
    chopped, and squeezed
    dry in paper towels
1½ cups (360 g) mayonnaise
2 Tbsp yellow mustard
2 Tbsp extra-virgin olive oil
1 Tbsp fresh lemon juice
Lavash or pita bread,
    for serving

In a medium saucepan, cover the potatoes with cold water and a generous pinch of salt and bring to a boil over high heat. Continue boiling for 15 to 20 minutes, or until a knife slides easily into the potatoes. Transfer the potatoes to a plate and let cool, then grate them using the large holes of box grater and set aside.

In a small saucepan, cover the eggs with cold water and bring to a rolling boil over high heat. Fill a small bowl with ice water. Boil the eggs for 3 minutes, then turn off the heat and let them stand for another 3 minutes. Transfer the eggs to the ice water. After a few minutes, gently crack the eggshells on the counter and use a spoon to remove the shells. Grate the eggs using the large holes of a box grater and set aside.

In a medium saucepan, cover the frozen peas and carrots with cold water and bring to a boil over high heat. Fill a medium bowl with ice water. Boil the peas and carrots for 2 minutes. Drain the peas and carrots, then add them to the ice bath and set aside.

Place the chicken, onion, garlic, salt, and pepper in a medium saucepan. Cover with water and bring to a boil over high heat. Continue boiling for about 20 minutes, or until the chicken is cooked through. Transfer the chicken to a cutting board and discard the onion and garlic. Shred the chicken with forks. Let cool to room temperature.

In a large bowl, combine the potatoes, eggs, peas and carrots, chicken, and pickles. Add the mayonnaise, mustard, oil, and lemon juice and mix thoroughly. Refrigerate the salad for at least 1 hour, or up to 24 hours, to let the flavors meld and combine before serving.

Serve the salad in a large bowl with lavash or pita bread, scooping it onto the bread. This salad gets better the longer it sits, and will keep in the refrigerator for 4 days.

CHILLED YOGURT AND HERB SOUP (AB DOOGH KHIAR) VEG

This soup is the antidote for hot weather and the easiest meal on a day when you cannot be bothered to put anything on the stove. After watering down thick yogurt into a soupy consistency, we add in cucumbers and herbs for freshness and texture, along with raisins and walnuts for a sweet and savory contrast. Ab doogh khiar can be a meal on its own or an appetizer when you're entertaining. This dish is not complete without ice cubes to guarantee a completely chilled soup, and pieces of crunchy bread to tear up and add to the liquid (tilit!), which turns them soft and chewy over time.

Serves 4

———

One 32 oz (907 g) container
  Greek yogurt
4 Persian cucumbers
  or 1 English cucumber,
  peeled and grated
1 small bunch green onions,
  white and green parts,
  finely chopped, plus more
  for serving
1 small bunch fresh mint,
  finely chopped (or 1 tsp
  dried mint), plus more for
  serving
1 Tbsp finely chopped fresh
  dill (or 1 tsp dried dill),
  plus more for serving
1 tsp fine salt
½ tsp black pepper
4 radishes, finely chopped
  (optional)
¼ cup (35 g) raisins
3 Tbsp chopped walnuts
Crunchy, dry lavash or pita
  bread, for serving

In a large bowl, combine the yogurt and 1 cup (240 ml) of water, stirring gently to avoid splashing. The yogurt should have the consistency of a thick soup—loose enough to drizzle off a spoon but not too watery. Add the cucumber, green onions, mint, dill, salt, and pepper and stir to incorporate—if entertaining, see the last paragraph for preparing additional toppings and ingredients.

When ready to enjoy, add the radishes, raisins, and walnuts, along with two handfuls of ice cubes. Serve with the bread for tilit.

If entertaining, set the radishes, raisins, and walnuts, along with additional green onions, mint, and dill and the bread, on a platter. Set out a bowl of ice cubes. Have your guests make their own bowl of soup with any combination of ingredients they would like, topping each with ice cubes and chunks of dried bread.

TOMATO AND EGG DROP SOUP (ESHKANE) VEG · GF

This is one of the oldest Iranian soups and while there are many variations on the recipe, this is our favorite. Bright tomatoes and savory eggplants become tender and flavorful with the addition of fresh herbs and a touch of fenugreek, which provides some mild bitterness that balances the dish. Fenugreek can be found at both Southwest Asian and South Asian grocers and online.

Serves 4

———

2 medium eggplants, washed, peeled, and cut into 2 in (5 cm) cubes

2 Tbsp fine salt

2 Tbsp extra-virgin olive oil

1 yellow onion, chopped

2 garlic cloves, minced

1 large russet potato, peeled and cut into 1 in (2.5 cm) chunks

1 Tbsp ground turmeric

½ tsp curry powder

½ tsp black pepper

2 Tbsp tomato paste

Red pepper flakes (optional)

4 large Roma tomatoes, chopped

⅓ cup (15 g) chopped fresh flat-leaf parsley

⅓ cup (15 g) chopped fresh cilantro

1 Tbsp dried fenugreek

6 cups (1.4 L) boiling water

2 large eggs

Fresh lemon juice, as needed

Hearty bread, for serving (optional)

Place the eggplant in a strainer, sprinkle with 1 Tbsp of salt, and shake it around to coat every piece. Set the strainer over a bowl and let stand for 20 to 30 minutes. Rinse the eggplant under cold water and leave to drain.

In a large pot, warm the oil over medium heat until glistening. Add the onion and cook, stirring occasionally, for about 5 minutes, or until translucent. Add the garlic, eggplant, and potato and cook, stirring occasionally, for 2 minutes. Add the turmeric, curry powder, black pepper, tomato paste, red pepper flakes (if using), and remaining 1 Tbsp of salt and cook, stirring occasionally, for 2 minutes. Add the tomatoes, parsley, cilantro, and fenugreek and stir thoroughly. Add enough of the boiling water to come almost to the top of the pot and bring to a vigorous boil over high heat. Turn the heat to medium and simmer for 30 minutes.

In a small bowl, whisk together the eggs and set aside.

Turn the heat to high and bring the soup to a boil again. Gradually start pouring the eggs into the pot using one hand and with the other hand, use a wooden spoon to constantly stir the mixture to create egg drops or ribbons of eggs. The whole process should take 2 minutes total. Taste the soup and season with salt, pepper, or lemon juice as needed.

Serve warm with hearty bread on the side, if desired. Eshkane will keep in an airtight container in the refrigerator for 3 days.

SPICED RED LENTIL SOUP (DAL ADASI) VGN · GF

Maman is from Abadan, a city in southern Iran, right on the Persian Gulf. Given the region's location, traders from across the continent brought spices and flavors to the country that weren't always found in Iranian cuisine. My mom's dal adasi is one of several dishes she makes that celebrate the unique flavors that came to her hometown from South Asia centuries ago, just like the Wonton Wrapper Sambusas (page 67). This dal is delectable on its own but also pairs beautifully with rice or bread.

Serves 4

——

1 medium russet potato, peeled

3 Tbsp extra-virgin olive oil, plus more for serving

1 small yellow onion, diced

3 garlic cloves, minced

1 Tbsp tomato paste

1 tsp ground turmeric

½ tsp curry powder

½ tsp ground cumin

¼ tsp red pepper flakes

½ tsp fine salt

1 cup (200 g) red lentils

3 cups (720 ml) hot or boiling water

Freshly ground black pepper

Warm rice or bread, for serving (optional)

In a small saucepan, cover the potato with water and bring to a boil over high heat. Continue boiling for 10 to 15 minutes, then use a knife to check if the potato is cooked. When the potato is tender, remove it from the water and set it aside to cool.

In a medium pot, warm the oil over medium heat until glistening. Add the onion and cook, stirring occasionally, for 5 to 7 minutes, or until translucent. Add the garlic and cook, stirring, for 1 minute, or until fragrant. Add the tomato paste, turmeric, curry powder, cumin, red pepper flakes, and salt and cook, stirring occasionally, for 2 to 3 minutes, or until the tomato paste is slightly darkened in color. Add the lentils and stir to coat them evenly in the spice mixture. Turn the heat to high, add the hot water, stir, and bring to a boil.

Meanwhile, grate the cooked potato using the large holes of a box grater, then add it to the lentil soup.

Once the soup is boiling, turn the heat to medium and let it simmer for 25 to 30 minutes, or until the mixture is thick and the lentils are cooked.

Serve warm with a drizzle of olive oil, a sprinkle of pepper, and rice or bread, if desired. Dal will keep in the refrigerator for 3 days.

CREAMY LEEK AND POTATO SOUP WITH TURMERIC AND CARROTS VEG · GF

One of the most fun parts of compiling these family recipes is learning the dishes that Maman picked up after emigrating from Iran. Maman learned this recipe while living in Greece and perfected it in the United States. Despite its straightforward ingredient list, this soup is decadent and velvety. The addition of shredded carrot lends a touch of color and texture to an otherwise silky broth. We love eating this with soup crackers or crusty bread, but it shines just as brightly on its own.

Serves 4

——

2 Tbsp extra-virgin olive oil, plus more for serving

3 large leeks, cut into ½ in (13 mm) pieces and thoroughly washed

2 medium russet potatoes, peeled and chopped

1 Tbsp fine salt

½ tsp black pepper

½ tsp ground turmeric

8 cups (2 L) vegetable broth or water

½ cup (25 g) shredded or finely chopped carrot (about 1 medium carrot)

1 cup (240 ml) heavy cream

Fresh lemon juice, for serving

In a medium pot, warm the oil over medium heat until glistening. Add the leeks and potatoes and sauté for 2 to 3 minutes, or until the leeks are translucent. Add the salt, pepper, and turmeric and stir to incorporate. Add the vegetable broth and bring to a boil over high heat. Continue boiling for 20 minutes, or until the leeks and potatoes are soft and tender. Remove from the heat.

Using an immersion blender or a countertop blender, blend the mixture until completely uniform with no chunks remaining. Return the pot to medium heat, add the shredded carrot, and cook for 10 minutes, or until the carrots are slightly softened. Stir in the heavy cream and season with salt and pepper.

Serve warm with a squeeze of lemon juice and a drizzle of oil. This soup keeps in the refrigerator for 4 days.

THREE BEAN AND NOODLE SOUP (ASH-E RESHTEH) VEG

Ash is a hearty vegetarian and protein-packed soup full of fresh greens. We eat it to celebrate Iranian New Year (the noodles represent good fortune), to send off loved ones on travels, and throughout the year to stay warm. In lieu of dried beans, you could easily use canned beans, which don't require any soaking or boiling. There are two special ingredients you can find in Southwest Asian grocers: kashk, which is salty whey, and reshteh, which are enriched flour noodles.

Serves 6 to 8

———

Vegetable oil

2 medium yellow onions, thinly sliced

1 Tbsp ground turmeric

½ tsp fine salt

¼ tsp black pepper

5 garlic cloves, thinly sliced

⅓ cup (15 g) dried mint

1 cup (160 g) dried white beans, soaked for at least 2 to 3 hours but ideally overnight

1 cup (180 g) dried chickpeas, soaked for at least 2 to 3 hours but ideally overnight

1 cup (180 g) dried pinto beans, soaked for at least 2 to 3 hours but ideally overnight

1 Tbsp ground cumin

Approx 8 cups (2 L) boiling water

1 cup (200 g) dried green lentils

1 bunch fresh chives, chopped

1 bunch fresh flat-leaf parsley, chopped

1 bunch fresh cilantro, chopped

1 bunch fresh dill, chopped

One 10 oz (280 g) package frozen chopped spinach

3 green onions (green parts only), thinly sliced

6 oz (170 g) enriched flour noodles (reshteh), broken into 1 in (2.5 cm) pieces

1 cup (220 g) liquid kashk (or Greek yogurt or sour cream), plus more for serving

In a medium sauté pan, warm 3 Tbsp of the oil over medium heat until glistening. Add the onions and cook, stirring occasionally, for about 20 minutes, or until golden. Add the turmeric, salt, and pepper and cook, stirring occasionally, for 2 minutes. Using a slotted spoon, transfer the onions to a bowl if serving right away or an airtight container if serving later. Do not clean the pan.

Add the garlic to the same pan, put it over medium heat, and cook, stirring occasionally, for 2 minutes; do not let it brown. Using a slotted spoon, transfer the garlic to a bowl if serving right away or an airtight container if serving later. Do not clean the pan.

Add the mint to the same pan, put it over medium heat, and cook, stirring, for 30 seconds. Immediately remove from the heat—you don't want the mint to burn. Pour the mint oil into a bowl if serving right away or an airtight container if serving later.

Drain the white beans, chickpeas, and pinto beans and combine in a medium pot. Cover the beans completely with water and add the cumin. Bring to a boil over high heat. Continue boiling for 5 minutes, then drain and rinse the beans.

continues →

THREE BEAN AND NOODLE SOUP (ASH-E RESHTEH)

In a large stockpot, warm 2 Tbsp of the oil over high heat until glistening. Add half of the prepared garlic, onions, and mint, followed by the drained beans. Add enough boiling water to fill the pot and submerge the beans and return to a rolling boil. Turn the heat to low and simmer for 1 hour. Add the lentils and simmer for 30 minutes. Stir in the chives, parsley, cilantro, dill, spinach, and green onions and simmer for 10 minutes, then add the noodles, turn the heat to high, and bring to a boil. Watch as the noodles boil, stirring occasionally, so they don't stick together. After 5 minutes, taste the noodles to make sure they're soft and turn the heat to low. Add the kashk and cook for another 10 to 15 minutes. Taste and lightly season with salt and pepper—kashk is very salty.

Serve ash in bowls, topped with the prepared garlic, onion, and mint and a drizzle of kashk. Ash keeps in the refrigerator for up to 1 week and can be frozen for up to 2 months.

CREAMY CHICKEN, BARLEY, AND VEGETABLE SOUP (SOUP-E JO)

The perfect pick-me-up, this comforting soup (pictured on page 95) tastes like a creamy version of chicken noodle soup. This was Maman's go-to remedy when we were sick and demonstrates how simple ingredients can turn into something special when simmered together. We make this year-round and love to serve it with heaps of fresh parsley on top, as well as with soup crackers.

Serves 4

———

2 large bone-in, skin-on chicken breasts or 4 bone-in, skin-on chicken thighs (about 1 lb [455 g] total)

1 medium yellow onion, peeled and trimmed

2 garlic cloves

1 Tbsp fine salt

1 tsp black pepper

½ cup (100 g) cracked barley

½ cup (70 g) finely diced or shredded carrot

2 cups (480 ml) whole milk or 1 cup (240 ml) heavy cream

3 Tbsp chopped fresh flat-leaf parsley

In a large pot, cover the chicken, onion, and garlic with 10 cups (2.4 L) of water. Add the salt and pepper, partially cover, and bring to a boil over high heat. Turn the heat to medium and simmer for 10 to 15 minutes, or until the chicken is cooked through. Strain the liquid, reserving both the liquid and the chicken but discarding the onion and garlic. This liquid is the broth that will be the base of your soup. Let the chicken cool, then shred it with two forks.

Return the broth to the pot and place over high heat. Add the cracked barley and carrot and bring to a boil. Turn the heat to medium, cover, and simmer for 30 to 40 minutes, or until the barley is cooked and tender. Add the milk and the shredded chicken. Stir to combine and continue simmering over medium heat for another 15 minutes to let the flavors combine. When there is 5 minutes remaining, add 2 Tbsp of the parsley and season with salt and pepper.

Sprinkle with the remaining 1 Tbsp of parsley and serve warm. Soup-e jo will keep in an airtight container in the refrigerator for 4 days.

HEARTY LAMB, BEAN, AND POTATO SOUP (ABGOOSHT) GF

This rustic soup (pictured on pages 98–99), consisting of delicious broth and goosht kubideh (mashed meat), is rich, savory, and a go-to for get-togethers. It's often paired with Torshi Liteh (page 70) and flatbread that's torn into pieces and soaked in the broth—tilit! The goosht kubideh can be added back into the soup but is also perfect on its own or in a wrap.

Serves 6

———

2 Tbsp vegetable oil

1 large yellow onion, diced, plus more raw sliced onion for serving

3 garlic cloves, minced

2 Tbsp tomato paste

2 dried bay leaves

1 cinnamon stick

1 Tbsp ground turmeric

1 Tbsp fine salt

½ tsp black pepper

½ tsp curry powder

½ tsp ground cumin

1 cup (180 g) dried chickpeas, soaked overnight

1 cup (160 g) dried white beans, soaked overnight

2 lb (910 g) bone-in lamb shank

2 large russet potatoes, peeled and quartered

Fresh lemon juice, for serving

Sangak or flatbread, warm, for serving

Iranian pickles or cornichons, for serving

Fresh basil, mint, tarragon, or other herbs, for serving (optional)

In a large stockpot, warm the oil over high heat until glistening. Add the onion and cook, stirring occasionally, for 5 minutes, or until translucent. Add the garlic and cook, stirring, for 30 seconds, or until fragrant. Add the tomato paste, bay leaves, cinnamon stick, turmeric, salt, pepper, curry powder, and cumin.

Drain the chickpeas and white beans, then add them to the pot, along with the lamb. Add 4 to 6 cups (960 ml to 1.4 L) of water, or more if there is room, until the meat and other ingredients are completely submerged. Bring to a boil, then partially cover, turn the heat to medium-low, and simmer for 1½ hours, or until the beans are tender but not too mushy! Add the potatoes and continue cooking for about 30 minutes, or until the lamb and potatoes are fully tender. Taste the broth and add fresh lemon juice, salt, and pepper as needed.

Remove the pot from the heat and, using a sieve or a ladle, separate the solids from the liquid into two large serving bowls. Remove and discard the lamb bones. Using a potato masher or immersion blender, mash the lamb, beans, and potatoes into a soft mixture. Taste both the solids and the broth and season as needed.

To serve, bring the soup and the mashed meat (goosht kubideh) to the table, along with warm bread, pickles, raw onions, and fresh herbs. The soup and the mashed meat will keep in the refrigerator for 5 days.

Rice & Pilafs

The Art of Tahdig

Rice (polo) is arguably the most important staple of Iranian cuisine. It's at the center of every table and paired with every single one of our stews and mains. Basmati rice, the most popular variety, has a subtle aroma and beautiful long grains that hold up to any cooking. Most often, our rice dishes include tahdig, the crisp crust that literally translates to "bottom of the pot." Some indescribable alchemy takes place when fluffy rice steams while a glorious crust forms around it. The bottom of the pot caramelizes the rice or other ingredient and turns it into something satisfyingly crunchy, nutty, and complex.

Iranian chefs are often judged on their ability to make a tahdig that is buttery with a satisfying crunch, without burning the bottom. I've spent many nights attempting to recreate Maman's tahdig in my small apartment, sometimes failing spectacularly—such as the time I nearly had to throw out the pot because the rice stuck to it—and sometimes getting it so good there's a fight for the last bite.

I started posting my mom's acrobatic tahdig flips and beautiful tahdigs on TikTok in 2020, never expecting them to reach—or resonate with—millions of people around the world. For Iranians, tahdig is an everyday staple, so the reactions surprised me. People have called her tahdig "drop-dead gorgeous" and "the most beautiful thing [they've] ever seen." The most common comments are demands for Maman's recipe. Now, our secret is out and you can make Maman's tahdig in the comfort of your own home. We'll even show you a few different styles of tahdig that are our favorites. We encourage you to test and experiment with these recipes—and your own—to find what works for you (and your stove!) and what you love best. We've made tahdig out of chicken wings and I've seen others make it with cabbage—the possibilities are endless.

Iranian food is typically prepared and served in generous portions, with hospitality being a core pillar of our culture. Tahdig is no exception; however, the importance of a large serving size can't be understated here. It's tricky to make tahdig with just one or two cups of rice in a saucepan, which often results in a flat, small pile of rice at the end. Part of the allure of tahdig is flipping over a big rice cake with a large crust, and it takes a few cups of rice to do that. Most of our recipes make enough rice to feed four people generously, which is a small enough amount to pull together on a weeknight. The rice will keep well in the refrigerator for several days, and tahdig can be re-fried in a pan, or you can make a new tahdig with leftover rice on top. After all, we're nothing if not resourceful.

Before we get into the recipes, you should know that this rice-cooking technique is a three-step process. And your pot is crucial: Tahdig is best made in a nonstick pot. If all you have is a cast-iron Dutch oven, you'll have to lower your heat, extend your cooking time, and be careful flipping such a heavy pan. The three steps include rinsing and soaking your rice, parboiling it, and then steaming it. We thoroughly rinse the rice in several changes of water, massaging it with our hands, to clean it of any dust, dirt, and debris, and repeating the process multiple times until the water runs clear. Next, we soak the rice in cold water for at least 15 minutes and up to 2 or 3 hours, which makes the grains plump up and cook more easily. The cooking process is similar to cooking pasta. In a large pot of salty boiling water, we parboil the rice for several minutes, which helps get rid of some of the excess starch and prevents the rice from sticking together. As Maman says, "You want your rice to dance." The rice is ready when the outside of the rice appears soft and cooked, while the inside is still firm; the rice should still have some bite to it. From there, put the rice in a strainer and thoroughly rinse it under cold water to immediately stop the cooking process. It's from this point on that you can choose what kind of tahdig you want to prepare, whether that's traditional rice tahdig, potato tahdig, tortilla tahdig, and so on. The next and final step is the steaming process.

At the bottom of the pot (the tah of your deeg!), warm some vegetable oil for a few minutes, then place the tahdig material of choice (raw potato slices, an uncooked tortilla, a thin layer of your parboiled rice, etc.) in the hot oil. Heap the parboiled rice on top in a mountain-like mound, avoiding the top edges of the pan, so the sides don't stick. With the handle of a long wooden spoon, make a few holes in the rice, going all the way to the bottom of the pot, to allow steam to escape. You can place some pats of butter, or a mix of oil and water, in the holes to make the rice buttery and delicious and prevent sticking. Next, you'll make a damkon (steamer) by wrapping the pot lid with clean paper towels or a clean dish towel. This crucial step creates a tight seal, traps the steam inside the pot, and prevents any condensation from dripping down the lid and making your rice (and tahdig!) mushy. After steaming over medium heat for 30 to 40 minutes, your rice is ready. Don't worry about the specifics just yet—we'll cover measurements and amounts in the recipes—and just consider this your "Tahdig 101" introduction.

If you attempt to make tahdig and the crust is soft, you might need higher heat at the start of cooking. If your crust is burnt, you can lower the heat for the first 5 minutes. Tahdig is both an art and a science, so keep trying and experimenting until you find what works!

Finally, here's one important thing to note, especially if Tahdig 101 spooked you: In recent years, Iranian rice cookers have become an incredibly versatile and helpful tool in making a great tahdig. They can consistently churn out beautiful tahdigs and perfect rice, without the parboiling step.

THREE TYPES OF TAHDIG:
RICE TAHDIG VGN · GF / TORTILLA TAHDIG VGN /
POTATO TAHDIG VGN · GF

Serves 4, with leftovers

———

RICE AND RICE TAHDIG

3 cups (600 g) long-grain
basmati rice

3 Tbsp fine salt

4 Tbsp vegetable oil

TORTILLA TAHDIG

1 or 2 large flour tortillas,
depending on the
size of the pan, cut
into 8 triangles

POTATO TAHDIG

¼ tsp ground turmeric
(optional)

Pinch of saffron (optional)

1 or 2 medium russet
potatoes, depending
on the size of the pan,
peeled and cut into
½ in (13 mm) thick rounds
and soaked in water for
a few minutes

To make the rice:

Rinse the rice in several changes of water, massaging it in a strainer or bowl until it runs clear. Let the rice soak in a large bowl of cold water for at least 15 minutes and up to 2 hours. Drain and set aside.

Bring a large pot (with a lid) of water to boil over high heat, then add the salt to flavor the rice while it cooks. Add the rice and cook for 8 to 10 minutes—stoves and pots have wildly different heat levels, so check the rice at the 4- or 5-minute mark to see how quickly it's cooking. Taste the rice for doneness: It should be soft on the outside but still slightly hard and uncooked in the middle. Drain the rice and rinse it with cold water to stop the cooking and rinse off excess starch. Set aside.

In a small bowl, mix 3 Tbsp of water with 2 Tbsp of the oil and set aside. You'll pour this into the rice right before steaming it.

Add the remaining 2 Tbsp of oil to generously coat the bottom of a medium pot. (You can wash the same one you boiled the rice in but go smaller if you can—you'll get a taller rice cake.) Place the pot over medium-high heat. Then, pick your tahdig…

To make the rice tahdig:

Place a thin layer of the parboiled rice on the bottom of the pot, gently patting it down to make a flat, even layer. Using a large spoon, gently layer the remaining parboiled rice on top, arranging it into a pyramid shape, so it doesn't stick to the sides of a pot.

To make the tortilla tahdig:

Arrange the tortilla triangles in the oil to cover the bottom of the pan. Using a large spoon, gently layer the parboiled rice on top, arranging it into a pyramid shape, so it doesn't stick to the sides of the pot.

continues →

THREE TYPES OF TAHDIG: RICE TAHDIG / TORTILLA TAHDIG / POTATO TAHDIG

To make the potato tahdig:

Add the turmeric and saffron (if using) to the warm oil and stir. Arrange the potato slices in a single layer on the bottom of the pot. If there is any extra space in the pan, cut any remaining potato slices into smaller pieces to fill in the gaps. Let the potatoes cook for 2 to 3 minutes to absorb the spices, then flip the potatoes over and make sure they still cover the bottom of the pot. Using a large spoon, gently layer the parboiled rice on top, arranging it into a pyramid shape, so it doesn't stick to the sides of the pot.

Make the damkon and steam the tahdig:

With the handle of a wooden spoon, make four holes in the rice, going all the way to the bottom of the pan (or close to it, if you are making tortilla or potato tahdig). Divide the reserved oil and water mixture among these holes. Wrap the pot lid with a tea towel or a few paper towels and cover tightly. Cook over medium-high heat for 5 minutes to let the tahdig crisp up. Turn the heat to medium and let the rice steam for 35 minutes, or until it is fully cooked and you can hear the tahdig moving on the bottom of the pan when you shake it. If you start to smell something burning, you've overcooked it!

The final step is optional but will help loosen tahdig that might be stuck to the pan. Fill the sink with 1 in (2.5 cm) of cold water and place the pot (with the lid on) in the sink. This will create steam that will quickly loosen the tahdig at the bottom. Remove the pot from the sink and remove the lid.

Place a large plate or platter on top of the pot and, mustering all the strength and confidence you have, quickly flip the rice over onto the plate in one smooth maneuver. If everything has worked out, you should have a gorgeous, crispy topped mountain of rice. If not, don't worry! It will still be delicious. Use a spatula to grab the tahdig stuck to the bottom and scatter it over the top of the rice.

Tahdig is best served immediately or while warm. We typically don't have leftovers because it's a precious commodity, but if you find yourself with leftover tahdig, the rice will still be delicious reheated on the stove in a sauté pan over medium-high heat with ½ Tbsp of oil, or in the microwave with 1 Tbsp of water so it steams.

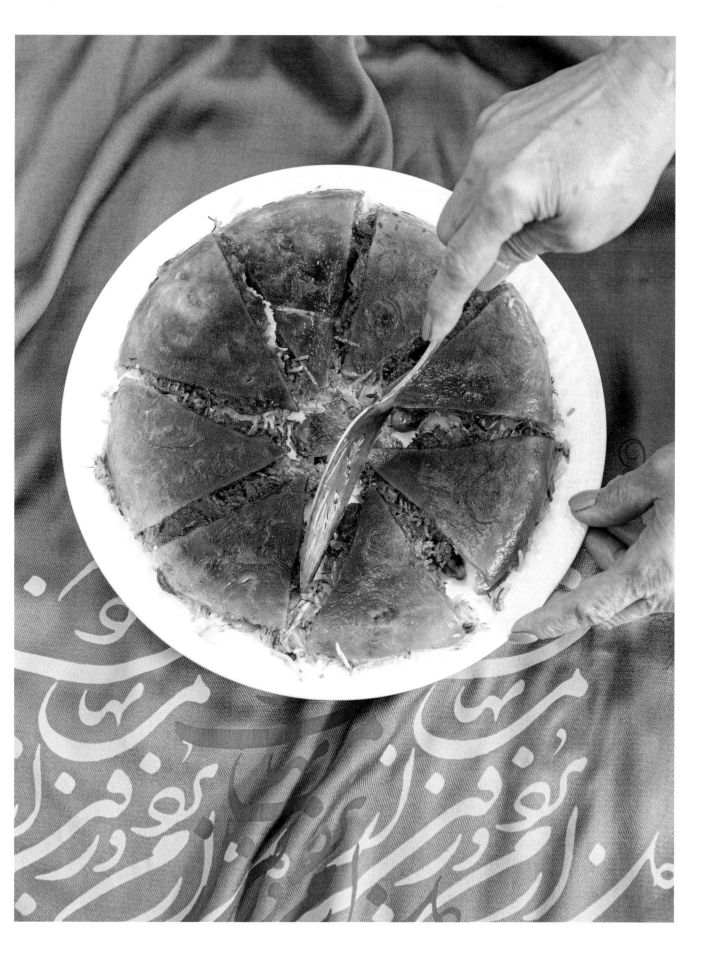

HERBED RICE WITH LIME (SABZI POLO) VGN · GF

This rice can be made with any combination of fresh herbs you have on hand and is perfect for using up any old herbs you might have in the refrigerator. We typically pair this rice with fish (try the Saffron Salmon with Ranch Dressing on page 148), which is a special holiday meal for Nowruz, Iranian New Year. Nowruz is the first day of spring, and the greens in this rice represent the regrowth and renewal that takes place in nature (and within ourselves) with every new year. Until writing this recipe, I assumed everyone ate this with fresh lime juice squeezed all over the top, but I learned this isn't customary. I suggest it anyway, as it really makes this herby rice shine.

Serves 4

——

3 Tbsp fine salt

3 cups (600 g) basmati rice, washed and rinsed thoroughly, soaked for at least 30 minutes, then drained

¼ tsp ground turmeric

1 tsp black pepper

1 cup (50 g) finely chopped fresh flat-leaf parsley leaves and tender stems

1 cup (50 g) finely chopped fresh cilantro leaves and tender stems

1 cup (40 g) finely chopped fresh dill

6 garlic cloves, finely chopped

4 Tbsp vegetable oil, for the tahdig

2 limes, for serving

Fill a large pot (with a lid) with water and bring to a boil over high heat. Once boiling, add the salt. Add the rice, turmeric, and black pepper, stirring to mix evenly. Cook the rice for 8 to 10 minutes, checking it at the 4- to 5-minute mark to see how quickly it's cooking. Taste one or two grains for doneness: The inside of the rice should be firm, while the outside of the grain should be cooked. With 1 minute of cooking left, stir in the parsley, cilantro, and dill.

Bring the pot to the sink and strain the rice. Rinse it thoroughly with cold water to stop the cooking and let it drain completely. Stir the chopped garlic into the drained rice, before steaming it and preparing your tahdig.

Follow the instructions on page 107 to make rice tahdig, preparing the water-oil mixture and your damkon to steam and crisp up the rice. The tahdig will turn a dark brown because of the herbs in the rice. Do not worry if it looks burnt; it will still taste amazing!

Cut the limes into wedges and serve alongside the warm rice, squeezing over the top for some brightness. Sabzi polo keeps in the refrigerator for up to 5 days.

TURMERIC RICE WITH TOMATOES AND POTATOES (ESTAMBOLI POLO) VGN · GF

This rice dish is Maman and Baba's comfort food, the kind of thing they make when it's just the two of them at home and they want something simple and easy. They make it at least once a month, sometimes on its own, sometimes prepared with a protein on the side (usually Sunday Chicken Stew, page 143), and always with thick yogurt to dollop on top. The rice turns a beautiful golden hue and has a lovely aroma thanks to turmeric, which pairs nicely with the juicy tomatoes and soft potatoes strewn throughout the pilaf. This recipe doesn't include a tahdig, but if you happen to overcook it, you'll still get some delicious crispy bits at the bottom.

Serves 4

———

3 Tbsp extra-virgin olive oil

1 large yellow onion, finely chopped

1 medium russet potato, peeled and cut into ½ in (13 mm) chunks

3 garlic cloves, minced

1 tsp ground turmeric

1 tsp ground cumin

1 tsp curry powder

Pinch of red pepper flakes (optional)

1 tsp fine salt

1 tsp black pepper

2 Tbsp tomato paste

2 cups (400 g) basmati rice, washed and rinsed thoroughly

6 Roma tomatoes, diced

3 cups (720 ml) hot or boiling water

Greek yogurt, for serving

In a large skillet with a lid, warm the oil over medium heat until glistening. Add the onion and cook, stirring often, for 5 minutes, or until lightly golden. Add the potato and cook, stirring occasionally, for 5 minutes, or until lightly softened—you're not trying to cook it through here! Add the garlic, turmeric, cumin, curry powder, red pepper flakes (if using), salt, and pepper. Stir in the tomato paste and cook for another 2 minutes, or until it darkens slightly. Add the rice and cook, stirring, for 2 minutes, so it can absorb the flavor and color of the spices. Add the tomatoes and hot water and stir to incorporate into the rice mixture. Bring to a boil and continue boiling for 10 to 20 minutes, or until the water almost completely evaporates from the top of the rice. Wrap the skillet lid with a tea towel or a few paper towels and cover tightly. Cook over low heat for 20 minutes, or until the water is completely absorbed and the rice is fully cooked.

Serve warm with the yogurt. Estamboli polo keeps in the refrigerator for 3 days and can be reheated on the stove or in the microwave with 2 Tbsp of water.

DILL AND FAVA BEAN RICE (SHEVEED BAGHALI POLO) VGN · GF

This dilly rice is a real treat and a great companion for our Garlicky Lamb Shank (page 160) or even on its own, given the protein from the beans. You can substitute lima beans, broad beans, or even edamame for the fava beans. You'll notice in this recipe, as in Sabzi Polo (page 111), that we add a touch of turmeric to the rice. This is to prevent the rice from looking too washed out or gray in contrast to the herbs. It imparts a touch of color without turning the whole pilaf yellow. We've included two cooking methods in this recipe, so you can make it with or without tahdig.

Serves 4

———

3 Tbsp fine salt

3 cups (600 g) basmati rice, washed and rinsed thoroughly, soaked for at least 30 minutes, then drained

¼ tsp ground turmeric

2 Tbsp dried dill

2 cups (80 g) finely chopped fresh dill

2 cups (455 g) frozen fava beans, thawed and drained

6 garlic cloves, finely chopped

Vegetable oil, for the tahdig

TORTILLA TAHDIG

1 or 2 large flour tortillas, depending on the size of the pan, cut into 8 triangles

POTATO TAHDIG

¼ tsp ground turmeric (optional)

Pinch of saffron (optional)

1 or 2 medium russet potatoes, depending on the size of the pan, peeled and cut into ½ in (13mm) thick rounds and soaked in water for a few minutes

Bring a large pot of water to a boil over high heat, then add the salt to flavor the rice while it cooks. Add the rice and turmeric, stirring to mix evenly, and cook for 8 to 10 minutes—stoves and pots have wildly different heat levels, so check the rice at the 4- or 5-minute mark to see how quickly it's cooking. Taste the rice for doneness: It should be soft on the outside but still slightly hard and uncooked in the middle. With 1 minute left, add the dried and fresh dill, along with the fava beans, stir, and let cook for that final minute. Drain the rice and rinse it with cold water to stop the cooking and rinse off excess starch. Set aside.

If you'd like to skip the tahdig:

Put the rice in a medium pot with a lid, then add the garlic. Set the pot over low heat and wrap the pot lid with a tea towel or a few paper towels and cover tightly. Let the rice steam for 15 to 20 minutes, or until cooked through. Serve warm.

If you'd like to make tahdig:

Follow the instructions on page 107 to make rice, tortilla, or potato tahdig (any of these will be delicious here!), stirring the garlic and a pinch of salt and pepper into the parboiled rice prior to steaming. This rice will keep in refrigerator for 3 days and can be reheated on the stove or in the microwave with 2 Tbsp of water.

SWEET AND SPICED LENTIL RICE (ADAS POLO) VEG · GF

This dish was Maman Bozorg's (my grandma's) favorite dish. Her name was Aghdas, so we would swap *adas*, the similar-sounding word for lentils, with her name and call it Aghdas polo instead of adas polo. Making this dish long after her passing feels meditative, like keeping an important part of her around with us. With protein from the lentils, it's substantial enough to eat on its own, but we'll sometimes prepare spiced ground beef (see Loobia Polo, page 129, for an example) to have on the side. Don't skip the sweet filling. It transforms the dish into something complex with contrasting flavors and textures. The steps in this recipe include a tahdig crust for the pilaf.

Serves 6

———

RICE

2 Tbsp fine salt,
 for seasoning the rice

¼ tsp ground turmeric

2 cups (400 g) basmati
 rice, washed and rinsed
 thoroughly, soaked for
 2 hours, then drained

1 cup (200 g) French lentils,
 soaked overnight then
 drained

Vegetable oil, for the tahdig

TORTILLA TAHDIG

1 or 2 large flour tortillas,
 depending on the
 size of the pan, cut into
 8 triangles

FILLING

3 Tbsp vegetable oil

2 small yellow onions,
 thinly sliced

1 tsp ground turmeric

¼ tsp curry powder

¼ tsp ground cumin

½ tsp fine salt

¼ tsp black pepper

1 cup (140 g) golden
 and/or brown raisins

8 to 10 Medjool dates,
 pitted and halved

⅓ cup (40 g) chopped
 walnuts (optional)

To make the rice:

Bring a large pot of water to a boil and add the salt to season. Once the water is boiling, add the turmeric and the rice. When the water returns to a boil, let it cook for 5 minutes, then stir in the lentils. Continue boiling for another 5 minutes, or until the rice is soft on the outside but still slightly hard and uncooked in the middle. Drain the rice and lentils and rinse them with cold water to stop the cooking and rinse off excess starch. Set aside.

Follow the instructions on page 107 to make rice or tortilla tahdig.

To make the filling:

In a sauté pan, warm the oil over medium heat until glistening. Add the onions and cook, stirring occasionally, for 5 minutes, or until translucent. Add the turmeric, curry powder, cumin, salt, and pepper and stir to coat the onions. Once the onions are lightly golden, stir in the raisins and dates and cook for 2 minutes, or until the raisins are slightly plumped. Stir in the chopped walnuts and cook for an additional 2 minutes.

When the polo is ready, you can serve it with the filling on the side, layer it on top, or alternate layers throughout.

VERMICELLI NOODLE PILAF WITH MEATBALLS (RESHTEH POLO)

This dish brings rice and noodles together in a beautiful pilaf. You can find toasted vermicelli noodles at most Southwest Asian grocers. We usually pair this polo with tiny meatballs, but it will be delicious with any entrée.

Serves 4

———

TOPPING
3 Tbsp vegetable oil
1 large yellow onion, thinly sliced
¼ tsp ground turmeric
1 tsp fine salt
Dash of ground cumin
½ cup (70 g) raisins
⅓ cup (40 g) chopped walnuts
10 Medjool dates, pitted and halved
Several dashes of ground cinnamon

RICE
2 Tbsp fine salt
Pinch of ground turmeric, plus more for the tahdig
1½ cups (300 g) basmati rice, washed and rinsed thoroughly, soaked for 1 hour, then drained
1 cup (200 g) toasted vermicelli noodles, broken into 1 in (2.5 cm) pieces
Vegetable oil, for the tahdig
Ground cinnamon, for the tahdig

POTATO TAHDIG
¼ tsp ground turmeric (optional)
Pinch of saffron (optional)
1 or 2 medium russet potatoes, depending on the size of the pan, peeled and cut into ½ in (13 mm) thick rounds and soaked in water for a few minutes

MEATBALLS
1 lb (455 g) ground beef
1 medium yellow onion, grated on the small holes of a box grater and excess water squeezed out
1 garlic clove, grated
1 tsp fine salt
½ tsp ground turmeric
¼ tsp black pepper
1 Tbsp vegetable oil
⅓ cup (80 ml) warm or boiling water
Pinch of ground saffron

To make the topping:
In a medium saucepan, warm the oil over medium heat until glistening. Add the onion and cook, stirring often, for 5 minutes, or until lightly golden. If your pan gets dry, add another glug of oil to prevent burning. Add the turmeric, salt, and cumin, then stir in the raisins. Turn the heat to low and continue cooking for 3 minutes, then add the walnuts and stir to incorporate. Stir in the dates and cinnamon and cook for 1 to 2 more minutes, or until warmed through. Keep warm.

To make the rice:
Bring a large pot of water to a boil over high heat, then add the salt and turmeric to flavor the rice while it cooks. Add the rice and cook for 8 to 10 minutes—stoves and pots have wildly different heat levels, so check the rice at the 4- or 5-minute mark to see how quickly it's cooking. Taste the rice for doneness: It should be soft on the outside but still slightly hard and uncooked in the middle. With 1 minute left, add the noodles and continue boiling for that final minute. Drain the rice and noodles and rinse them with cold water to stop the cooking and rinse off excess starch. Set aside.

continues →

VERMICELLI NOODLE PILAF WITH MEATBALLS (RESHTEH POLO)

To make the potato tahdig:

Follow the instructions on page 108 to make potato tahdig, adding the par-boiled rice in batches and sprinkling the cumin and cinnamon between each layer.

To make the meatballs:

In a medium bowl, combine the beef, onion, garlic, salt, turmeric, and pepper. Grabbing small, cherry-size pieces of the mixture, form it into meatballs and arrange them on a tray or plate.

In a large frying pan, warm the oil over medium heat until glistening. Add the meatballs and cook for 2 to 3 minutes, then start shaking the pan, so the meatballs roll around (no need for a spatula, they'll get smushed). Continue cooking and shaking the pan for 2 to 3 minutes, or until the meatballs are browned all over. Add the warm water, along with the ground saffron, and cook for 2 to 3 minutes, or until the water evaporates.

To serve, layer the rice, meatballs, and topping on a platter.

SWEET JEWELED RICE (SHIRIN POLO) VEG · GF

Shirin polo, also known as javaher polo (jeweled rice), is a treat bursting with flavor and color. It's the star dish at weddings and parties for good reason. Carrot Jam brings sweetness and barberries add sourness, while almonds and pistachios provide crunch. You can serve this alongside Sunday Chicken Stew (page 143), made without tomato paste, so it doesn't overpower the polo.

Serves 4 to 6

———

1 cup (250 g) barberries, rinsed thoroughly and soaked in cold water for 30 minutes, then drained

2 Tbsp fine salt

¼ tsp ground turmeric

2 cups (400 g) basmati rice, washed and rinsed thoroughly, soaked for 2 hours, then drained

Vegetable oil, plus more for saffron rice (optional)

Pinch of ground saffron, bloomed in warm water, plus more for topping the rice (optional)

1 Tbsp granulated sugar

½ cup (60 g) slivered almonds

2 Tbsp unsalted butter

¼ cup (30 g) slivered pistachios

¼ cup (60 ml) rosewater

1 cup (8 oz) Carrot Jam (page 36)

Line a tray with paper towels and pour the drained barberries on top. Feel around to remove any thorny stems or stones and pat the barberries dry.

Bring a large pot of water to a boil over high heat, then add the salt and turmeric to flavor the rice while it cooks. Add the rice and cook for 8 to 10 minutes—stoves and pots have wildly different heat levels, so check the rice at the 4- or 5-minute mark to see how quickly it's cooking. Taste the rice for doneness: It should be soft on the outside but still slightly hard and uncooked in the middle. Drain the rice and rinse it with cold water to stop the cooking and rinse off excess starch. Set aside.

Follow the instructions on page 107 to make rice tahdig.

While the rice is steaming, in a small frying pan, warm 2 Tbsp of the oil over medium heat until glistening. Add the steeped saffron, reserving 1 tsp, followed by the barberries and sugar, and cook, stirring constantly, for 1 minute, then immediately remove from the heat.

Bring a small saucepan of water to a boil over high heat. Add the almonds and continue boiling for 5 minutes. Drain the almonds and rinse with cold water, then dry them with paper towels.

In a small frying pan, melt the butter over medium heat. Add the blanched almonds and cook, stirring constantly, until lightly golden; don't let them turn brown. Remove the almonds from the pan so they don't continue cooking.

In a small bowl, combine the pistachios and rosewater and let soak for at least 10 minutes, then drain.

continues →

SWEET JEWELED RICE (SHIRIN POLO)

When the rice is cooked, before you flip it, scoop several spoonfuls of rice from the top of the pot into a small bowl. Add a glug of oil and the reserved 1 tsp of bloomed saffron and mix thoroughly until the rice is bright orange, adding more saffron as needed.

To serve, flip the rice onto a platter and crack into the tahdig with a spatula. Top the "broken" tahdig and the white rice with the carrot jam, barberries, almonds, pistachios, and saffron rice. Shirin polo will keep in an airtight container in the refrigerator for 3 days.

SAFFRON SHRIMP PILAF (MEYGOO POLO) GF

This is a special polo from Maman's home region in Iran. The shrimp turn a vibrant yellow from saffron and sit on pillows of soft rice layered with spiced raisins, softened onions, and crunchy walnuts. Maman precooks the shrimp with lemon juice and saffron to get rid of any fishy smells, but you can skip this step.

Serves 4

———

2 Tbsp fine salt plus 1 tsp and more as needed

2 cups (400 g) basmati rice, washed and rinsed thoroughly, soaked for 2 hours, then drained

Vegetable oil, for cooking the shrimp and for the tahdig

¼ tsp ground saffron, plus a pinch

1 lb (455 g) peeled and deveined shrimp, tails removed

2 Tbsp fresh lemon juice

1 large yellow onion, sliced

½ tsp black pepper

1 tsp ground turmeric

¼ tsp ground cinnamon

½ cup (70 g) golden raisins

½ cup (70 g) black raisins

½ cup (60 g) chopped walnuts

Fill a large pot with water and bring to a boil over high heat, then add 2 Tbsp of the salt to flavor the rice while it cooks. Add the rice and cook for 8 to 10 minutes—stoves and pots have wildly different heat levels, so check the rice at the 4- or 5-minute mark to see how quickly it's cooking. Taste the rice for doneness: It should be soft on the outside but still slightly hard and uncooked in the middle. Drain the rice and rinse it with cold water to stop the cooking and rinse off excess starch. Set aside.

Follow the instructions on page 107 to make rice, tortilla, or potato tahdig.

While the rice is cooking, make the shrimp. This first step is optional: In a large frying pan, warm 1 Tbsp of oil and the pinch of saffron over medium heat until glistening. If you're cooking shrimp in batches, add a pinch of saffron for each batch. Add the shrimp and cook for 1 minute, or until they release their water. Add the lemon juice and stir thoroughly. Remove the pan from the heat. Transfer the shrimp to a strainer, rinse with cold water, and pat dry.

Clean the frying pan, then add 2 Tbsp of oil and the remaining ¼ tsp of saffron and warm over medium heat until glistening. Add the shrimp in an even layer and cook for about 1 minute, or until they turn lightly pink. Flip the shrimp and cook for 2 more minutes. Transfer the shrimp to a covered platter and set aside; wash the pan.

In the same pan, heat 1 Tbsp of oil over high heat. Add the onion and a pinch of salt and cook, stirring occasionally, for about 10 minutes, or until golden and soft. Add the remaining 1 tsp of salt, along with the pepper, turmeric, and cinnamon. Add the golden and black raisins and cook, stirring, for 1 to 2 minutes, or until slightly plumped. Add the walnuts and cook, stirring, for 1 more minute. Remove from the heat.

Once the rice is finished, flip it onto a platter and break the tahdig with a spatula. Cover the tahdig and rice with the shrimp, onion, and raisin mixture—you could also alternate layers of rice and layers of the mixture here.

Serve warm. Meygoo polo will keep in the refrigerator for up to 4 days.

CRUNCHY BAKED SAFFRON RICE WITH CHICKEN (TAHCHIN) GF

Tahchin is like a casserole with a very special twist: Every slice has tahdig! The contrast between the crunchy bottom and the soft rice studded with chicken is a delight.

Serves 6

———

2 large chicken breasts (about 1 lb [455 g] total)

1 small yellow onion, peeled

2 garlic cloves

2 tsp fine salt plus 2 Tbsp, for seasoning the rice

¼ tsp black pepper

¼ tsp ground turmeric

2 cups (400 g) basmati rice, washed and rinsed thoroughly, soaked for 1 hour, then drained

1 large egg plus 2 large egg yolks

¼ cup (60 g) Greek yogurt

7 Tbsp (110 ml) vegetable oil

1 to 2 tsp ground saffron, bloomed in 3 Tbsp water, plus more as needed

1 tsp rosewater

¼ cup (60 g) barberries, for serving (optional)

In a small pot, combine the chicken, onion, garlic, 1 tsp of the salt, the pepper, and the turmeric. Cover with water and bring to a boil over high heat. Continue boiling for 15 minutes, or until the chicken is fully cooked. Drain the chicken and let it cool, then pat it dry and shred it using two forks.

Preheat the oven to 375°F (190°C).

While the chicken is cooking, make the rice. Bring a large pot of water to a boil over high heat, then add 2 Tbsp of the salt to flavor the rice while it cooks. Add the rice and cook for 5 minutes. The rice should still have bite to it; you'll need to undercook this because the rice continues cooking in the oven. Drain the rice and rinse it with cold water to stop the cooking and rinse off excess starch. Set aside.

In a large bowl, whisk together the egg and egg yolks. Add the yogurt, 5 Tbsp of the oil, the bloomed saffron, the rosewater, and the remaining 1 tsp of salt and stir to combine. Add the rice and mix until evenly combined. If your rice isn't bright yellow, bloom an additional 1 tsp of saffron in 1 Tbsp of water and add it to the mixture.

Spread the remaining 2 Tbsp of oil in a 9 x 13 in (23 x 33 cm) glass baking dish. Spread half of the rice in the bottom of the dish, pressing and smoothing it with a spatula. Arrange the chicken evenly across the top of the rice. Top with the remaining rice, pressing and smoothing it with a spatula and then patting it down. With the tip of a knife, make several incisions all the way into the tahchin to allow steam to escape. Cover the top of the dish with parchment paper, then wrap the dish with a layer of aluminum foil.

Bake for 30 minutes, then rotate the baking dish and turn the oven temperature to 350°F (180°C). Bake for 1 hour, then check the dish to see if the bottom has formed a tahdig-style crust. If not, continue baking, checking for the crust every 15 minutes. When the bottom is uniformly golden brown, remove it from the oven.

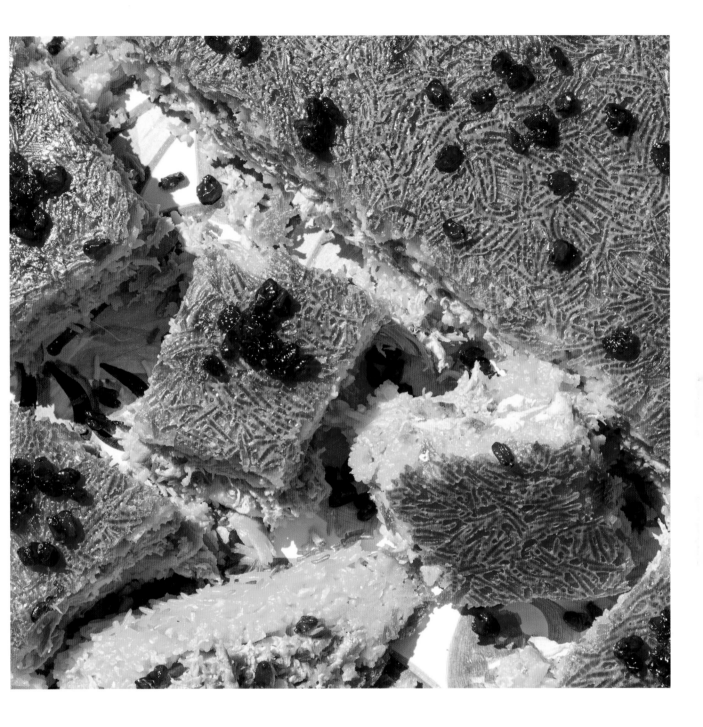

Let the tahchin cool for 5 minutes, then remove the foil and parchment paper. You can try to bravely do a tahdig flip using a tray or serve it in slices directly from the baking dish.

Serve tahchin warm with a sprinkle of barberries. Tahchin keeps in the refrigerator for up to 4 days and in the freezer for up to 2 months.

GREEN BEAN AND BEEF PILAF (LOOBIA POLO) GF

This pilaf is a meal all on its own! Loobia polo is commonly served with Mast-o Khiar (page 53) and Salad Shirazi (page 77)—we love mixing them together for a creamy, savory combination in every bite.

Serves 4 to 6

———

2 Tbsp vegetable oil, plus
   more for the tahdig

1 lb (455 g) green beans,
   trimmed and cut into
   1 in (2.5 cm) pieces

1 large yellow onion, chopped

1 lb (455 g) ground beef

3 garlic cloves, minced

3 Tbsp tomato paste

1 cinnamon stick

2 tsp ground turmeric

3 Tbsp fine salt for seasoning
   the rice, plus 1 tsp

1 tsp black pepper

2 pinches of ground saffron
   plus about 1 tsp (optional)

1 cup (240 ml) warm or
   boiling water

3 cups (600 g) basmati
   rice, washed and rinsed
   thoroughly, soaked for
   1 hour, then drained

1 or 2 medium russet
   potatoes, depending
   on the size of the pan,
   peeled and cut into ½ in
   (13 mm) thick rounds
   and soaked in water for
   a few minutes

Pinch of ground cardamom
   (optional)

In a medium sauté pan, warm 1 Tbsp of the oil over medium heat until glistening. Add the green beans and cook, stirring occasionally, for 10 minutes, or until golden and slightly softened. Remove from the pan and set aside. Do not clean the pan.

In the same pan, warm the remaining 1 Tbsp of oil over medium heat until glistening. Add the onion and cook, stirring occasionally, for 10 minutes, or until lightly golden. Add the beef and garlic and cook, stirring occasionally, for 5 minutes, or until the beef is lightly browned. Stir in the tomato paste and cook for 2 minutes, or until it is darkened in color. Add the cinnamon stick, 1 tsp of the turmeric, 1 tsp of the salt, the pepper, and 1 pinch of the saffron (if using). Add the warm water, stir, and bring to a boil. Turn the heat to medium, cover, and cook for 15 to 20 minutes, or until cooked through. Remove the meat from the pan, setting it aside on a plate. If there is still liquid in the pan, ladle it into a bowl and set it aside.

Bring a large pot of water to a boil over high heat, then add the remaining 3 Tbsp of salt, the remaining 1 tsp of turmeric, and 1 pinch of the saffron (if using) to flavor the rice while it cooks. Add the rice and cook for 8 to 10 minutes—stoves and pots have wildly different heat levels, so check the rice at the 4- or 5-minute mark to see how quickly it's cooking. Taste the rice for doneness: It should be soft on the outside but still slightly hard and uncooked in the middle. Drain the rice and rinse it with cold water to stop the cooking and rinse off excess starch. Set aside.

Follow the instructions on page 108 to make potato tahdig, but instead of piling the entire amount of parboiled rice on top of the potatoes, make layers with the rice, green beans, and beef. After the first tahdig layer of potatoes, add one-third of the rice, followed by one-third of the green beans, and one-third of the beef. Sprinkle each layer with pinches of saffron and cardamom (if using). Repeat with the remaining rice, green beans, and beef until the pot is full. If there was leftover liquid from cooking the meat, pour a few spoonfuls on top of the rice. Continue cooking the rice according to the tahdig recipe.

Serve warm. Loobia polo will keep in the refrigerator for up to 4 days.

DOLMA STUFFED PEPPERS (DOLMEH FELFEL) GF

Dolma (stuffed grape leaves) are a treat, but filling and rolling individual grape leaves is an ordeal. Instead of using grape leaves, we love using the filling to stuff bell peppers or on its own as a pilaf, which is just as delicious. This recipe calls for split chickpeas, which are the key ingredient in Split Chickpea Stew with Crunchy Potatoes (page 139). These are chickpeas that are husked and split in half. They are commonly used in South Asian stews and soups and are readily available at most South Asian grocers.

Serves 6

——

1 Tbsp fine salt for seasoning
the rice, plus 1 tsp

¾ tsp ground turmeric

1 cup (200 g) basmati
rice, washed and rinsed
thoroughly, then drained

½ cup (112 g) split chickpeas,
washed thoroughly

3 Tbsp extra-virgin olive oil

1 large yellow onion,
grated on the small
holes of a box grater

2 garlic cloves, minced

8 oz (230 g) ground beef

1 Tbsp tomato paste

Pinch of ground saffron

½ tsp black pepper

1 Tbsp chopped fresh
flat-leaf parsley
(or 1 tsp dried parsley)

1 Tbsp chopped fresh
cilantro (or 1 tsp dried)

1 Tbsp dried tarragon

1 Tbsp dried rosemary

1 Tbsp dried dill

3 Tbsp fresh lemon juice

4 to 6 large bell peppers

Bring a large pot of water to a boil over high heat, then add 1 Tbsp of the salt and ¼ tsp of the turmeric. Add the rice and cook for 8 to 10 minutes—stoves and pots have wildly different heat levels, so check the rice at the 4- or 5-minute mark to see how quickly it's cooking. Taste the rice for doneness: It should be soft on the outside but still slightly hard and uncooked in the middle. Drain the rice and rinse it with cold water to stop the cooking and rinse off excess starch. Set aside.

In a small saucepan, combine the split chickpeas with 3 cups (720 ml) of water and a pinch of salt and bring to a boil over high heat, watching carefully so they don't boil over. Continue boiling for 10 minutes, or until the split chickpeas are tender but not mushy. Drain and set aside.

In a large frying pan, warm 1 Tbsp of the oil over high heat until glistening. Add the onion and cook for about 5 minutes, or until translucent. Add the garlic and cook for 1 minute. Add the beef, stirring and breaking down any chunks with a wooden spatula. Turn the heat to medium, then add the tomato paste, saffron, pepper, parsley, cilantro, tarragon, rosemary, dill, the remaining 1 tsp of salt, and the remaining ½ tsp of turmeric and stir to fully incorporate. Add 1 Tbsp of the lemon juice and cook for 2 to 3 minutes, then remove from the heat.

In a large bowl, combine the beef, rice, and chickpea mixtures and stir with a spoon to fully incorporate.

Cut the tops off the bell peppers. Remove and discard the stems but reserve the tops. Scoop out the seeds and as much of the membranes as possible. Fill the bell peppers two-thirds full with the beef mixture. Use toothpicks to secure the pepper tops to the bottoms. Place the peppers, tops on and upright, in a medium pot, then add 1 cup (240 ml) of water, along with the remaining 2 Tbsp of lemon juice and the remaining

2 Tbsp of olive oil around the peppers. Put the pot over high heat, cover, and bring the water to a rolling boil. Turn the heat to medium-low and continue cooking for 45 minutes to 1 hour, or until the peppers have softened and the insides look fully cooked.

Serve warm. Dolmeh felfel will keep in the refrigerator for 3 days.

Main Dishes & Stews

Hearty Tomato and Eggplant Stew (Yatimche)
VGN · GF — 135

Eggs-plant: Garlicky Eggplant and Eggs (Mirza Ghasemi)
VEG · GF — 136

Split Chickpea Stew with Crunchy Potatoes (Gheymeh)
VGN · GF — 139

Sweet and Sour Pomegranate and Walnut Stew (Fesenjoon)
VGN · GF — 140

Sunday Chicken Stew (Khorak-e Morgh)
GF — 143

Spicy and Sour Tamarind Fish Stew (Ghalieh Mahi)
144

Iranian Shrimp Scampi (Escampi)
147

Saffron Salmon with Ranch Dressing
GF — 148

Eggplant, Okra, and Beef Stew (Khoresh Bademjan)
GF — 151

Green Herb, Beef, and Kidney Bean Stew (Ghormeh Sabzi)
GF — 152

Herbed Beef and Celery Stew (Khoresh Karafs)
GF — 155

Stovetop Kabob (Tas Kabob)
GF — 156

Spaghetti with Tahdig (Espaghetti)
159

Garlicky Lamb Shank
GF — 160

HEARTY TOMATO AND EGGPLANT STEW (YATIMCHE) VGN · GF

Yatimche means "little orphan," and this dish was named as such because of its humble ingredients. Iranian culinary tradition tends to value elaborate dishes, such as Shirin Polo (page 121), but dishes like yatimche are the ones that people make often, seek relief in, and prepare to feel nourished and satisfied. We hope that this dish becomes one of your comfort foods. Feel free to experiment with how you serve it and what you serve it with. I love it over rice, and sometimes add feta or chili crisp, while my parents slather it on bread.

Serves 4

———

3 medium eggplants, peeled and cut into 1 in (2.5 cm) chunks

1½ tsp fine salt for salting the eggplants, plus 1 tsp for cooking the eggplant

2 Tbsp extra-virgin olive oil

1 large yellow onion, thinly sliced

3 garlic cloves, minced

4 medium tomatoes, quartered

1 Tbsp dried mint

1 tsp ground turmeric

½ tsp black pepper

2 cups (480 ml) warm or boiling water

1 Tbsp fresh lemon juice

Warm bread or rice, for serving (optional)

Put the eggplant in a strainer set over a bowl and generously coat it with 1½ tsp of the salt. Let sit for at least 30 minutes, then rinse the eggplant and pat it dry.

In a medium pot, warm the oil over medium heat until glistening. Add the onion and cook, stirring occasionally, for 5 minutes, or until translucent. Add the eggplant and continue cooking, stirring occasionally, for 4 to 6 minutes, or until lightly softened. Add the garlic, tomatoes, mint, turmeric, pepper, and the remaining 1 tsp of salt and stir to incorporate. Add the warm water and lemon juice and bring to a boil over high heat. Turn the heat to low, cover, and simmer for 30 minutes, or until the eggplant and tomatoes are completely soft and most of the water has evaporated. Taste and season with salt and pepper as needed.

Serve warm with bread or rice. Yatimche will keep in the refrigerator for 4 days.

EGGS-PLANT: GARLICKY EGGPLANT AND EGGS (MIRZA GHASEMI) VEG · GF

The warmth and flavors of this dish are excellent any time of day. The combination of runny egg yolks with a turmeric-spiced eggplant and tomato mash is out-of-this-world delicious, but feel free to experiment with some additional spiciness or different ways to prepare the eggs. Poached eggs are delicious here, as are scrambled.

Serves 2 to 4

——

6 medium eggplants, stems trimmed but intact and flesh pricked all over with a fork

2 Tbsp vegetable oil, plus more for brushing the eggplant

4 garlic cloves, minced

1 tsp ground turmeric

1 tsp fine salt

½ tsp black pepper

Pinch of red pepper flakes (optional)

3 medium Roma tomatoes, chopped and seeded

2 to 4 large eggs (1 per serving)

Chopped fresh herbs, such as cilantro and parsley, for serving

Warm lavash, pita bread, or rice, for serving

Put the eggplant in a casserole-style baking dish and brush the skin with oil.

If you have a grill, set it to 450°F (230°C). Put the eggplant directly on the grill racks and grill, turning, for several minutes on each side until evenly charred. Alternatively, preheat the oven to 400°F (200°C) and bake the eggplant, turning twice, so all sides char evenly, for 20 to 25 minutes.

Once the eggplant is charred all over, return it to the baking dish, cover the dish with plastic wrap, and let stand for 5 to 7 minutes to steam the insides and make the skin easier to remove. Using the tip of a knife, gently remove the skin from the eggplant and discard. Put the eggplant flesh on a cutting board and chop it finely until it is mashed with no big chunks remaining.

In a medium frying pan, warm the 2 Tbsp of oil over medium heat until glistening. Add the mashed eggplant and cook, stirring occasionally, for 7 to 10 minutes, or until lightly golden. Add the garlic, turmeric, salt, pepper, and red pepper flakes (if using) and cook for 2 minutes. Add the tomatoes and cook, stirring frequently, for 5 to 7 minutes, or until the water from the tomatoes has evaporated and the mixture has thickened and pulled away from the pan around the edges.

You can either fry the eggs separately in a pan or cook them in the eggplant and tomato mixture: Make wells in the mixture and crack the eggs directly into them. Season the eggs with salt and pepper, then turn the heat to low and cook for about 5 minutes, or until the whites are set but the yolks are still runny.

Sprinkle with the fresh herbs and serve alongside warm bread or rice. Mirza ghasemi will keep in the refrigerator for 2 days.

SPLIT CHICKPEA STEW WITH CRUNCHY POTATOES (GHEYMEH) VGN · GF

This fun stew is topped with french fries, but you can use store-bought French's potato sticks instead. Maman insists the mushroom stems be removed and set aside for future use, because the mushroom caps look like beautiful flowers in this dish.

Serves 5

———

Vegetable oil, for cooking

1 lb (455 g) white mushrooms, stems removed

1 lemon, halved

1 cup (225 g) split chickpeas, washed thoroughly

1½ tsp fine salt

1¼ tsp ground turmeric

Extra-virgin olive oil, for cooking

1 large yellow onion, diced

2 garlic cloves, minced

1 Tbsp tomato paste

½ tsp black pepper

½ tsp ground cumin

1 cinnamon stick

2 large russet potatoes, peeled, cut into thin fries, and soaked for 30 minutes

Warm basmati rice, for serving

In a medium frying pan, warm 2 Tbsp of the vegetable oil over high heat until glistening. Add the mushrooms and squeeze the juice from half of the lemon into the pan. Cook the mushrooms, flipping once, for 2 to 3 minutes on each side, or until both sides are lightly golden. Transfer the mushrooms to a paper towel–lined plate and set aside.

In a medium saucepan, cover the split chickpeas with water. Add ½ tsp of the salt, ¼ tsp of the turmeric, and a glug of olive oil and bring to a boil over high heat. Continue boiling for 5 minutes, watching carefully so it doesn't overflow. Drain the split chickpeas and rinse with cold water.

In a medium pot, warm 2 Tbsp of the vegetable oil over medium heat until glistening. Add the onion and cook, stirring occasionally, for about 5 minutes, or until translucent. Stir in the split chickpea mixture, garlic, tomato paste, pepper, cumin, and cinnamon stick, along with the remaining 1 tsp of salt and the remaining 1 tsp of turmeric. Add enough water (2 to 4 cups [480 to 960 ml]) to cover and bring to a rolling boil over high heat. Turn the heat to medium, cover, and simmer for 30 minutes, or until the split chickpeas are tender. Add the mushrooms and squeeze the juice from the remaining lemon half into the stew. Taste the stew to make sure the split chickpeas are cooked through and season as needed. Turn the heat to low and gently simmer for another 30 minutes.

Meanwhile, drain the potatoes and pat them dry. Line a platter with paper towels and put it nearby. Heat ½ in (13 mm) of the vegetable oil in a medium frying pan over medium-high heat. The oil is ready when bubbles form steadily around the handle of a wooden spoon dipped in the oil. Working in batches, add the potatoes and fry, turning occasionally, for 3 to 4 minutes, or until light golden and crisp. Transfer the potatoes to the paper towel–lined platter and immediately season with salt. Continue frying the remaining potatoes, adjusting the heat as needed.

Serve gheymeh with the rice and potatoes on the side to prevent them from getting soggy. Gheymeh will keep in the refrigerator for 3 days.

SWEET AND SOUR POMEGRANATE AND WALNUT STEW (FESENJOON) VGN · GF

This stew is decadent, and it will surprise you. It's both sweet and tart, and its deep brown, gravy-like color comes from letting ground walnuts and pomegranate molasses bubble up and slowly simmer. Be patient with it: If it's not the dark, velvety brown pictured here, let it continue cooking until you get there—slow simmering is essential for all our stews! Fesenjoon can be served on its own, with fried tofu, or alongside sautéed chicken.

Serves 4 to 6

———

3 cups (360 g) raw, unsalted walnuts

3 Tbsp granulated sugar plus 1 tsp

½ medium butternut squash, peeled and chopped

1 cup (240 ml) pomegranate molasses

½ tsp ground turmeric

½ tsp fine salt

¼ tsp black pepper

¼ tsp ground cinnamon

4 cups (960 ml) warm or boiling water

Warm basmati rice, for serving

In a food processor, combine the walnuts and 1 tsp of the sugar and grind into fine crumbs that resemble grains of sand. Transfer the mixture to a bowl. Wipe out the food processor, then add the butternut squash and process until finely ground into tiny bits (or you can use a box grater to do this by hand).

In a dry medium pot, toast the walnut mixture over medium heat, stirring constantly, for about 5 minutes, or until the walnuts release some of their natural oils and become fragrant. Add the squash, pomegranate molasses, turmeric, salt, black pepper, cinnamon, and warm water and stir to combine. Turn the heat to low, cover, and simmer, stirring every 10 minutes to prevent burning, for 45 minutes. Stir in the remaining 3 Tbsp of sugar. Continue simmering the stew for another 30 minutes, or until it's a deep, dark brown color and some of the walnut oil pools on top. The oil can be removed (my mom's preference), or you can leave it as is for more flavor. Taste and season with salt and pepper as needed.

Serve fesenjoon warm with rice. Fesenjoon will keep in the refrigerator for 3 days.

SUNDAY CHICKEN STEW (KHORAK-E MORGH) GF

This stew is a one-pot wonder, the perfect meal for a cozy Sunday or whenever you want to make something simple that still tastes amazing. When Maman Bozorg was in her late seventies and into her eighties, she ate this nearly every day—you can eat it that often and not tire from it. It's especially tasty with Estamboli Polo (page 112). You can vary any of the vegetables here, swapping in seasonal ingredients or your favorites.

Serves 4

——

1 Tbsp vegetable oil

1 lb (455 g) bone-in, skin-on chicken thighs or drumsticks

1 medium yellow onion, diced

3 garlic cloves, minced

2 dried bay leaves

1 cinnamon stick

1 Tbsp tomato paste

1 Tbsp ground turmeric

1 tsp fine salt

½ tsp black pepper

2 to 3 cups (480 to 720 ml) warm or boiling water

2 Tbsp fresh lemon juice

6 to 8 new potatoes

1 cup (140 g) medium diced carrots

1 cup (120 g) chopped celery

5¼ oz (150 g) green beans, trimmed

Warm basmati rice, for serving

In a medium pot, warm the oil over medium heat until glistening. Add the chicken and cook for 3 minutes, then flip it over to cook the other side. Immediately add the onion and cook, stirring occasionally, for about 5 minutes, or until translucent. Add the garlic, bay leaves, cinnamon stick, tomato paste, turmeric, salt, and pepper and cook, stirring occasionally, for 2 to 3 minutes, or until the tomato paste has deepened in color. Add enough of the warm water to cover the mixture, followed by the lemon juice, and stir to incorporate. Add the potatoes, carrots, celery, green beans, and a pinch of salt and bring to a rolling boil over high heat. Turn the heat to medium, cover, and simmer for 45 minutes to 1 hour, or until the chicken is completely cooked.

Serve warm with rice. Khorak-e morgh keeps in the refrigerator for up to 4 days.

SPICY AND SOUR TAMARIND FISH STEW (GHALIEH MAHI)

This is another special dish from Maman's home, southern Iran. Fenugreek, tamarind paste, and jalapeños combine to create a tart, bitter, and complex stew with a nice kick. Because the potency of tamarind paste varies by brand, start with 1 Tbsp and continue tasting the stew and adding more until you get to a nice tart flavor. We fry the fish separately from the stew. You can serve it on the side (my preference) or place the fillets on top of the stew (Maman's preference), which allows it to take on the stew's amazing flavors but means it loses its crunch.

Serves 4

———

5 Tbsp (75 ml) vegetable oil

1 medium yellow onion, chopped

2 bunches fresh cilantro, finely chopped

1 bunch fresh flat-leaf parsley, finely chopped

1 bunch green onions, finely chopped

5 garlic cloves, minced

1 Tbsp dried fenugreek

4 Tbsp all-purpose flour

1 tsp ground turmeric

1 tsp fine salt

½ tsp black pepper

½ tsp curry powder

2 cups (480 ml) warm or boiling water

1 to 3 Tbsp tamarind paste

4 large cod fillets (about 2 lb [910 g] total)

1 jalapeño pepper, finely chopped, or ¼ tsp red pepper flakes

Warm basmati rice, for serving

In a medium pot, heat 1 Tbsp of the oil over high heat until glistening. Add the onion and cook, stirring occasionally, for about 5 minutes, or until translucent. Add the cilantro, parsley, green onions, garlic, and fenugreek and stir to combine. Add 1 Tbsp of the flour, along with the turmeric, salt, pepper, and curry powder, and cook, stirring often, for 2 minutes. Add the warm water and 1 Tbsp of the tamarind paste, then stir to incorporate and bring to a boil. Turn the heat to medium, partially cover, and simmer for 30 minutes to 1 hour, or until the stew reaches your desired thickness.

Meanwhile, prepare the fish. Pat the fillets dry with paper towels, then season with salt and pepper. Put the remaining 3 Tbsp of flour in a small bowl. Dredge the fillets in the flour, shaking them to get rid of any excess flour.

In a large frying pan, warm the remaining 4 Tbsp of oil over medium-high heat for 2 to 3 minutes. Add the fish and fry for about 3 minutes, or until golden on the bottom. Flip the fish and fry for 3 more minutes, or until golden on the other side.

When the stew is the thickness you desire, taste and season with salt and pepper. If the stew isn't tart enough, add tamarind paste, 1 Tbsp at a time.

Serve the fish alongside the stew or place the fillets directly on top. Serve warm with rice. Ghalieh mahi will keep in the refrigerator for 3 days.

IRANIAN SHRIMP SCAMPI (ESCAMPI)

Maman noticed how much we liked shrimp scampi at Italian restaurants and put her own twist on it—with turmeric, of course! We call it escampi, adding the "eh" sound that often comes before words that begin with s in Farsi. This recipe is simple and versatile: You can sauté the shrimp with saffron like we do in Meygoo Polo (page 125), add heavy cream to the sauce for richness (we do this often), or make this with chicken instead of shrimp.

Serves 4 to 6

———

1½ Tbsp fine salt for the pasta water, plus ¾ tsp

¼ tsp ground turmeric

One 16 oz (455 g) package linguine or any long pasta

3 Tbsp extra-virgin olive oil

3 Tbsp unsalted butter

4 garlic cloves, minced

1 tsp ground saffron, bloomed in 2 Tbsp boiling water

¼ cup (60 ml) dry white wine

2 lb (910 g) large shrimp, cleaned thoroughly and tails removed

1 lemon, zested and juiced

2 Tbsp chopped fresh flat-leaf parsley, plus more for serving

Grated Parmesan cheese, for serving

Bring a medium pot of water to a boil, then add 1½ Tbsp of the salt and the turmeric. Add the linguine and cook according to the package instructions until al dente. Reserve 1 cup (240 ml) of the pasta water for the sauce. Drain the pasta and place it back in the pot.

Meanwhile, in a medium frying pan over medium heat, combine 1 Tbsp of the olive oil, the butter, garlic, bloomed saffron, and the remaining ¾ tsp of salt. Cook, stirring occasionally, for 1 minute, or until the garlic is fragrant. Add the wine and cook for 2 minutes, or until the wine is reduced by half. Add the shrimp and cook, without stirring but watching it closely, for about 2 minutes, or until pink on the bottom. Flip the shrimp and cook for 1 more minute, or until pink on the other side. Stir in the lemon zest, lemon juice, and chopped parsley, then remove from the heat.

Add the shrimp and saffron butter to the linguine, along with the remaining 2 Tbsp of olive oil, and use tongs to toss and combine, adding pasta water, ¼ cup (60 ml) at a time, until you have a glossy sauce.

Sprinkle with the Parmesan and more parsley and enjoy warm. Escampi will keep in the refrigerator for 3 days.

SAFFRON SALMON WITH RANCH DRESSING GF

The unlikely marriage of saffron and ranch dressing feels like the essence of *Maman and Me*. It is culinary alchemy achieved by experimenting with new flavors in a new home country. Maybe in another thirty years, we'll have saffron ranch on grocery shelves! We top our salmon with peppers, mushrooms, walnuts, and tomatoes, arranging the tomatoes on top to resemble fish scales. We make this every Nowruz, our new year, with Sabzi Polo (page 111).

Serves 5

———

One 2 lb (910 g) skin-on salmon fillet

1 tsp fine salt

½ tsp black pepper

½ tsp ground saffron, bloomed over 2 ice cubes

2 limes, halved

4 Tbsp extra-virgin olive oil

1 large yellow onion, diced

1 red bell pepper, cut into 1 in (2.5 cm) pieces

1 yellow bell pepper, cut into 1 in (2.5 cm) pieces

1 orange bell pepper, cut into 1 in (2.5 cm) pieces

8 oz (230 g) baby bella (cremini) mushrooms, sliced

6 garlic cloves, minced

1 tsp ground turmeric

½ tsp curry powder

¼ tsp red pepper flakes

¼ cup (30 g) chopped walnuts

2 to 3 Tbsp ranch dressing

2 cups (280 g) cherry tomatoes, halved

Sabzi Polo (page 111), for serving

Put the salmon on a baking sheet and top with the salt, pepper, and bloomed saffron. Squeeze the limes over the salmon, then drizzle with 2 Tbsp of the oil. Cover the salmon and place in the refrigerator to marinate for 30 minutes.

While the fish marinates, in a medium frying pan, warm the remaining 2 Tbsp of oil over medium heat. Add the onion and cook, stirring occasionally, for 5 minutes, or until translucent. Add the bell peppers and cook, stirring occasionally, for 5 minutes, or until slightly softened. Add the mushrooms and cook, stirring occasionally, for 5 minutes, then add the garlic, turmeric, curry powder, red pepper flakes, and walnuts and cook, stirring occasionally, for 2 minutes, or until fragrant. Remove from the heat.

Preheat the oven to 350°F (180°C). Take the fish out of the refrigerator and let it come to room temperature.

Once the fish is at room temperature, bake it for 20 minutes, then remove from the oven and check for doneness—the fish should be opaque pink and flake easily when poked with a fork. Let the fish cool on the baking sheet for 30 minutes.

Set the oven's broiler to low.

Using a pastry brush or the back of a spoon, spread the ranch dressing on top of the salmon. With a spoon, carefully place a uniform layer of the onion-pepper-mushroom mixture on top of the salmon. Place the cherry tomatoes, one by one and cut-side down, on top of this mixture. Sprinkle a pinch of salt over the top. Place the salmon under the broiler for 5 minutes, watching it closely. When the tomatoes start bursting and changing color—and before they burn!—take the salmon out of the oven.

Serve warm with the sabzi polo. The salmon will keep in the refrigerator for 3 days.

EGGPLANT, OKRA, AND BEEF STEW (KHORESH BADEMJAN) GF

Every time I visit my family, I ask Maman to make this stew. The combination of tender beef, soft eggplant, and tart tomatoes forms a deliciously rich stew, with chewy, springy okra adding texture throughout. You'll notice in our beef-based stew recipes that there's a step to blanch the meat. This eliminates some of the gaminess but is totally optional.

Serves 4

———

4 to 6 small eggplants, peeled with the tops left intact

3 Tbsp fine salt for coating the eggplants, plus 2 tsp

1 to 1½ lb (455 to 680 g) stew beef chunks

7 Tbsp (105 ml) vegetable oil

1 large yellow onion, diced

3 garlic cloves, minced

1 Tbsp tomato paste

1 cinnamon stick

1 tsp ground turmeric

½ tsp black pepper

½ tsp curry powder

3 to 4 cups (720 to 960 ml) warm or boiling water

One 16 oz (455 g) package frozen okra, thawed

½ cup (70 g) cherry tomatoes

Rice with tahdig (page 107)

Put the eggplants in a strainer set over a bowl and generously coat them with 3 Tbsp of the salt. Let sit for at least 30 minutes, then rinse the eggplants and pat them dry.

Blanch the beef (optional): Put the beef in a large pot, cover it with water, and bring to a boil over high heat. Continue boiling for 2 to 3 minutes, then drain the beef and rinse it with cold water. Wash the pot.

In the same pot, heat 2 Tbsp of the oil over medium heat until glistening. Add the onion and cook, stirring occasionally, for 5 minutes, or until translucent. Add the beef back into the pot and cook, stirring occasionally, for 3 to 5 minutes. Add the garlic, tomato paste, cinnamon stick, turmeric, pepper, curry powder, and the remaining 2 tsp of salt and cook, stirring occasionally, for 2 minutes, or until the tomato paste darkens. Add enough of the warm water to cover the meat and bring to a boil over high heat. Turn the heat to medium, cover, and simmer for 1 hour.

Meanwhile, cook the eggplant: In a large frying pan, warm the remaining 5 Tbsp of oil over medium heat until glistening. Using tongs, add the whole eggplants and cook, turning as needed, for 3 minutes on each side, or until light golden brown all over. Use the tongs to transfer the eggplants to a strainer set in the sink or a bowl and let drain to remove any excess oil.

When the beef is fully cooked, use the tongs to layer the eggplants on top of the stew. Add the okra, along with the cherry tomatoes, on top. Turn the heat to high and bring to a boil. Turn the heat to medium-low, cover, and simmer for 30 minutes.

Serve warm with rice, pouring the stew juices over your tahdig. Khoresh bademjan will keep in the refrigerator for 4 days.

GREEN HERB, BEEF, AND KIDNEY BEAN STEW (GHORMEH SABZI) GF

This popular stew combines beef, kidney beans, fresh herbs, dried fenugreek, and tart limoo omani (dried limes) for a sour and savory dish that gets better the longer it sits. Limoo omani can be found in most Southwest Asian grocers. Consider using a food processor to finely chop the parsley and cilantro, which will give you the best result. When you serve this alongside rice, pour the sour juices and cooked-down herbs all over your tahdig and let it sit to soften the tahdig and infuse it with the stew's tart flavors.

Serves 4

———

1½ lb (680 g) stew beef chunks

3 Tbsp vegetable oil

1 large yellow onion, diced

2 garlic cloves, minced

1 cinnamon stick

1 tsp ground turmeric

1 tsp fine salt

½ tsp black pepper

1 cup (160 g) dried red kidney beans, soaked for at least 30 minutes but ideally overnight, or one 15½ oz (440 g) can red kidney beans

4 whole limoo omani (or 3 Tbsp fresh lemon juice)

2 medium bunches fresh flat-leaf parsley, finely chopped

2 medium bunches fresh cilantro, finely chopped

2 medium bunches fresh chives, finely chopped

1 Tbsp dried fenugreek

Fresh lemon juice (optional)

Rice with tahdig (page 107)

Blanch the beef (optional):
Place the beef in a medium pot, cover it with water, and bring it to a boil over high heat. Continue boiling for 2 to 3 minutes, then drain the beef and rinse it with cold water. Wash the pot.

In the same pot, heat 1 Tbsp of the oil over medium heat until glistening. Add the onion and cook, stirring occasionally, for 5 to 7 minutes, or until translucent. Add the meat and cook, stirring occasionally, for 2 minutes. Add the garlic and cook, stirring occasionally, for 1 minute, or until fragrant. Add the cinnamon stick, turmeric, salt, and pepper.

Drain the red kidney beans (drain and rinse the canned beans, if using), then add to the stew, along with the limoo omani and enough water to cover. Turn the heat to high and bring to a rolling boil. Turn the heat to medium, cover, and simmer for 30 minutes.

Meanwhile, prepare your herbs: In a medium sauté pan, heat the remaining 2 Tbsp of oil over medium heat until glistening. Add the parsley, cilantro, chives, and fenugreek and cook, stirring occasionally, for about 10 minutes, or until the water from the herbs has evaporated. Continue cooking for 5 more minutes, or until the herbs are wilted (they should be dark green but not burned!) and fragrant, then remove from the heat.

Stir the fried herbs into the stew, turn the heat to low, and gently simmer, covered, for another 30 minutes, or until the meat is tender and the beans are cooked through. If the stew is watery, let it simmer, uncovered, for another 20 minutes. Taste and season with salt, pepper, and lemon juice as needed. Ghormeh sabzi will keep in the refrigerator for 4 days.

HERBED BEEF AND CELERY STEW (KHORESH KARAFS) GF

Cooked celery is the star of this stew. The celery retains some bite thanks to a quick frying and takes on the flavors of the fresh parsley and cilantro that form the base of this dish. While there's a decent amount of sabzi (green herbs) in this stew, it tastes quite different from Ghormeh Sabzi (page 152), because it doesn't have the acidity from the dried limes or the bitterness from the fenugreek. The first step of boiling and rinsing the meat is optional but is something Maman likes to do.

Serves 4

——

1½ lb (680 g) stew
    beef chunks

4 Tbsp vegetable oil

1 medium bunch celery, cut
    into 1 in (2.5 cm) pieces

1 medium bunch fresh
    flat-leaf parsley, finely
    chopped

1 medium bunch fresh
    cilantro, finely chopped

1 Tbsp dried mint

1 yellow onion, finely
    chopped

2 garlic cloves, minced

1 cinnamon stick

1 tsp ground turmeric

1 tsp fine salt

½ tsp black pepper

Fresh lemon juice (optional)

Warm basmati rice,
    for serving

Blanch the beef (optional):

Place the beef in a small saucepan, cover it with water, and bring it to a boil over high heat. Continue boiling for 2 to 3 minutes, then drain the beef and rinse it with cold water.

In a large frying pan, warm 2 Tbsp of the oil over medium heat until glistening. Working in batches, add the celery and cook, stirring occasionally, for 5 to 7 minutes, or until the edges are lightly golden. Add the parsley and cilantro and cook, stirring, until the water from the herbs has evaporated. Stir in the mint, then remove from the heat.

In a medium pot, heat the remaining 2 Tbsp of oil over medium heat until glistening. Add the onion and cook, stirring occasionally, for 5 to 7 minutes, or until translucent. Add the beef and cook for 2 to 3 minutes, or until lightly browned on the outside. Add the garlic, cinnamon stick, turmeric, salt, pepper, and just enough water to barely cover. Turn the heat to high and bring to a rolling boil. Turn the heat to medium-low, cover, and simmer for 30 to 40 minutes, or until the beef is tender. Stir in the fried celery and herb mixture and continue simmering for another 30 minutes. If the stew is watery, let it simmer, uncovered, for another 20 minutes. Taste and season with salt, pepper, and lemon juice as needed.

Serve with rice. Khoresh karafs will keep in the refrigerator for 4 days.

STOVETOP KABOB (TAS KABOB) GF

Kabob, typically skewered meat cooked over a fire, is an Iranian staple and the dish that's found in most Iranian restaurants. This stovetop version, reminiscent of meatloaf and topped with chunky potatoes and tomatoes, is easier and better suited for making at home—the entire recipe comes together in one pan. We sometimes add one or two sliced Granny Smith apples to the pan for a sweet and tart contrast.

Serves 4

———

1 lb (455 g) ground beef

1 large yellow onion, grated on the large holes of a box grater

2 garlic cloves, grated on the small holes of a box grater or a Microplane

1 tsp ground turmeric

1 tsp fine salt

½ tsp black pepper

½ tsp curry powder

1 lemon, halved

2 medium russet potatoes, peeled and cut into 1 in (2.5 cm) chunks

6 Roma tomatoes, halved crosswise

1 or 2 Granny Smith apples, cut into ½ in (13 mm) pieces (optional)

Warm basmati rice, for serving

Sumac, for serving

In a medium bowl, use your hands to gently combine the ground beef, onion, and garlic, being careful not to overmix it. Add the turmeric, salt, pepper, and curry powder, mixing until evenly combined.

In a large, preferably nonstick, frying pan with a lid, press the ground beef mixture into a large circular patty. Using a spatula, divide the patty into fourths and then into eighths. Place the pan over medium heat and squeeze half a lemon over it, then cover and cook for 7 to 10 minutes, or until some of the moisture from the meat evaporates. Use the spatula to flip the wedges of kabob, then immediately arrange the potatoes on top of the kabob and sprinkle with a pinch of salt. Arrange the tomatoes on top of the potatoes, then add the apples on top (if using), sprinkle with a pinch of salt, and squeeze the remaining half lemon on top. Cover and cook for 15 to 20 minutes, or until the potatoes are fork-tender. If the potatoes are still firm, continue cooking for another 5 to 10 minutes.

Serve warm with rice and sprinkle sumac on both the rice and the kabob. Tas kabob keeps in the refrigerator for up to 3 days.

SPAGHETTI WITH TAHDIG (ESPAGHETTI)

Iranian spaghetti might feel familiar, but as usual, there's a twist: We make spaghetti tahdig. Like escampi, this recipe takes its name from the Italian term, but we add an *e* before the *s*, as the word would be pronounced in Farsi. This sauce is meatier, thicker, and less wet than a typical red-sauce spaghetti, and we serve it with generous dollops of Greek yogurt (on the side or mixed in) for creamy tanginess.

Serves 4

——

4 Tbsp vegetable oil

1 large yellow onion, chopped

1 lb (455 g) ground beef

4 garlic cloves, minced

2 Tbsp tomato paste

8 oz (230 g) white
    mushrooms, sliced

2 Tbsp chopped fresh flat-
    leaf parsley (or 1 Tbsp
    dried parsley)

2 Tbsp chopped fresh cilantro
    (or 1 Tbsp dried cilantro)

1½ Tbsp fine salt, for
    seasoning the pasta,
    plus 1 tsp

½ tsp black pepper

¼ tsp red pepper flakes

⅔ cup (160 ml) hot or boiling
    water

½ tsp ground turmeric

One 16 oz (455 g) package
    bucatini or thick spaghetti

Greek yogurt, for serving

In a large frying pan, heat 2 Tbsp of the oil over medium heat until glistening. Add the onion and cook for about 5 minutes, or until translucent. Add the beef and cook, breaking up any chunks with a wooden spatula, for about 5 minutes, or until browned. Add the garlic, tomato paste, mushrooms, parsley, cilantro, 1 tsp of the salt, the black pepper, and red pepper flakes and cook, stirring occasionally, for 2 more minutes, or until the tomato paste deepens in color. Add the hot water and decrease the heat to low. Simmer for 20 minutes, or until the mixture has thickened.

Meanwhile, bring a large pot (with a lid) of water to a boil over high heat. Add the turmeric and the remaining 1½ Tbsp of salt to season the pasta while it cooks. Add the pasta and cook according to the package instructions until al dente. Drain the pasta, rinse it with cool water to stop the cooking, and drain again. Rinse and dry the pot you used to cook the pasta.

In the same pot, warm the remaining 2 Tbsp of oil over medium heat until glistening. Place a layer of the pasta on the bottom of the pan, followed by a layer of the meat mixture, another layer of pasta, and then another layer of meat, repeating until you've used all the pasta and meat. Using two forks, try to carefully mix the meat and noodles together without disrupting the bottom layer.

Make the damkon and steam the tahdig:

Wrap the pot lid with a tea towel or a few paper towels and cover tightly. Cook over medium-high heat for 10 minutes, then turn the heat to low and let the pasta steam for 25 minutes, or until you can hear the tahdig moving on the bottom of the pot when you shake it. If you smell something burning, you've overcooked it.

Flip your spaghetti tahdig and enjoy with spoonfuls of Greek yogurt on the side. Espaghetti will keep in the refrigerator for 4 days.

GARLICKY LAMB SHANK GF

This is a great weekend meal, the kind of dish that lovingly simmers over the course of a few hours. Lamb doesn't require a ton of ingredients to taste amazing, but a lengthy cooking time is the secret to making it soft, tender, and falling off the bone. We usually serve these lamb shanks with the Dill and Fava Bean Rice (page 115), but it would go wonderfully with most rice dishes and pilafs in this book. Make sure to pour the juices from the bottom of the pot all over your rice and tahdig.

Serves 4 to 6

——

4 lamb shanks (about
    4 to 5 lb [1.8 to 2.3 kg]
    total)

2 Tbsp vegetable oil

1 large yellow onion, peeled
    and ends removed

8 garlic cloves, peeled

2 bay leaves

1 cinnamon stick

1 tsp ground turmeric

1 tsp ground saffron,
    bloomed in 2 Tbsp
    boiled water

1 tsp fine salt

½ tsp black pepper

3 Tbsp unsalted butter,
    cut into small pieces

Rice with tahdig (page 107)

Blanch the lamb (recommended):
Put the lamb in a large pot, cover it with water, and bring to a boil over high heat. Continue boiling for 2 to 3 minutes, or until you see foam on the top. Drain the lamb, rinse it with cold water, and pat it dry. Wash and dry the pot.

In the same pot, warm the oil over medium heat until glistening. Add the lamb shank and cook for about 5 minutes, or until the bottom is browned. Flip the lamb, then add the onion, garlic, bay leaves, cinnamon stick, turmeric, saffron, salt, and pepper. Add enough water to cover the top of the lamb shanks, then turn the heat to high and bring to a rolling boil. Turn the heat to medium, cover, and simmer for at least 2 hours. Check the lamb with a fork—the meat should fall off the bone. If it isn't that tender yet, continue simmering for another 15 to 20 minutes, or until completely tender. Remove from the heat and arrange the shanks on a serving dish, topping with the butter while they're still steaming hot. Strain the juices from the pot and pour into the serving dish, discarding the solids. Taste and season with salt and pepper.

Serve warm with rice. Lamb shanks will keep in the refrigerator for up to 4 days.

Drinks

CHILLED CHIA, LIME, AND ROSE DRINK (SHARBAT-E TOKHME SHARBATI) VGN · GF

This chia, lime, and rose combination is one of many Iranian sharbats, sweet and fragrant syrup-based drinks that are popular in warmer weather. It has a fun, thick consistency from the chia seeds that, over time, suspend midway through the drink. Sharbat is like a natural sports drink, delicious after a workout or helpful after a hangover. The chia seeds and limes help with hydration, as well as digestion.

Serves 2

———

SIMPLE SYRUP

½ cup (100 g) granulated
    sugar

SHARBAT

¼ cup (45 g) chia seeds

4 limes, juiced

¼ cup (60 ml) rosewater

To make the simple syrup:

In a small saucepan, bring the sugar and 1 cup (240 ml) of water to a rolling boil over high heat, occasionally stirring with a wooden spoon. Once the sugar is dissolved, remove from the heat and let cool for 15 minutes.

To make the sharbat:

Pour the cooled simple syrup into a pitcher or large reusable container. Add 4 cups (960 ml) of water and the chia seeds and stir thoroughly to agitate the chia seeds and evenly distribute them in the mixture. Put the sharbat in the refrigerator for 30 minutes, stir to mix the chia seeds again, and then refrigerate for another 30 minutes.

When ready to serve the sharbat, add the lime juice and rosewater, stir, and enjoy immediately.

VINEGARY CUCUMBER AND MINT TONIC (SEKANJEBIN) VGN · GF

The foundation of this sharbat is a mint simple syrup spiked with vinegar. Maman serves this with a massive romaine lettuce leaf in the glass, which I found odd growing up, but her friends (and now mine) love it and it looks quite stunning. It's also common to dunk lettuce directly into the syrup, which can be an unexpected party appetizer or refreshing afternoon snack. I think cucumbers and watermelon would also make for incredible dippers in this decadent, vinegary syrup. You can change the ratio of syrup to water, depending on how sweet you'd like the drink; the ratio here is a good starting point. For a refreshing cocktail, pour a dash of vodka or white rum into this sharbat. This will make about 2 cups (480 ml) of mint simple syrup, which you can use for additional servings of the tonic or it will keep in the refrigerator for up to 2 months.

Serves 1

———

MINT SIMPLE SYRUP

2 cups (400 g) granulated sugar

1 bunch fresh mint, stems and leaves

¼ cup (60 ml) white vinegar

TONIC

Cold still or sparkling water

1 Persian cucumber, finely grated

Ice cubes, as needed

Fresh mint or romaine lettuce, for garnish (optional)

Romaine lettuce leaves, for serving or dunking in syrup (optional)

To make the mint simple syrup:

In a small saucepan, bring the sugar and 1 cup (240 ml) of water to a rolling boil over high heat, occasionally stirring with a wooden spoon. When the sugar is completely dissolved, add the mint stems and leaves and continue boiling, stirring occasionally, for 10 to 15 minutes, or until the syrup thickens enough to coat the back of a spoon. Add the white vinegar, stir, and remove from the heat. Let the syrup cool for 15 minutes, then strain to remove the mint stems and leaves.

To make 1 tonic:

In a glass, combine 2 Tbsp of syrup and 1 cup (240 ml) of cold still or sparkling water and stir to dissolve. Add heaping spoonfuls of grated cucumber and ice if needed. Garnish with a sprig of mint or a fresh romaine leaf and enjoy. Repeat to make more tonics or use the remaining syrup for dunking romaine lettuce leaves. The mint simple syrup will keep in an airtight container in the refrigerator for up to 2 months.

CANTALOUPE AND ROSE SMOOTHIE VGN · GF

This isn't your typical smoothie loaded with multiple fruits and perhaps some leafy greens. It's simple, refreshing, and ideal when cantaloupe is in season. Maman grew up drinking this and made it for us every summer. This recipe is easily scalable, depending on the size of the fruit: Use 1 Tbsp of granulated sugar and 1 tsp of rosewater for every cup (140 g) of cantaloupe. This could also be turned into a cocktail with the addition of light rum or vodka.

Serves 4

———

1 medium cantaloupe,
    peeled and cut into 1 in
    (2.5 cm) chunks
1 to 2 Tbsp granulated sugar
1 cup (240 ml) cold water
2 tsp rosewater
½ cup (110 g) ice cubes
Fresh lemon juice (optional)
Fresh mint sprigs, for garnish
    (optional)

Taste the cantaloupe for sweetness. If it's very ripe and sweet, skip adding sugar until after blending. Put the cantaloupe in a blender, then add 1 to 2 Tbsp of the sugar, depending on the fruit's sweetness and your taste. Add the cold water, rosewater, and ice and blend until the mixture is smooth with no chunks of cantaloupe remaining. Taste for flavor, sweetness, and acidity and add sugar, rosewater, and lemon juice, 1 tsp at a time, as needed.

Serve immediately with a sprig of fresh mint for garnish.

FIZZY YOGURT SODA (DOOGH) VEG · GF

Doogh is a savory yogurt-based drink that pairs perfectly with any red meat–based dishes, any kind of kabob, including Stovetop Kabob (page 156), or an afternoon mezze platter. Thick yogurt, spiked with mint and salt, is made fizzy with the addition of club soda or sparkling water, almost as if Cooling Cucumber Yogurt (page 53) were a bubbly drink. You can make doogh with still water, but carbonation takes the drink to a new level. Be warned: It's commonly believed that doogh can put you into a deep sleep (and research shows lactic acid can improve your sleep quality!), so much so that we don't make any plans for after drinking it.

Serves 2

——

1 cup (240 g) Greek yogurt

1 tsp fine salt

½ tsp dried mint

2 cups (480 ml) club soda
    or sparkling water

Ice cubes, for serving

In a pitcher, combine the yogurt, salt, and mint. Slowly pour in the club soda and gently stir with a spoon until there are no lumps remaining. Serve immediately in cups with ice.

POMEGRANATE MOLASSES SPRITZ VGN · GF

Over the decades that we've been making our beloved Sweet and Sour Pomegranate and Walnut Stew (page 140), which features pomegranate molasses as a star ingredient, we'd usually eat the sticky, sour molasses right off our hands if we ever spilled it. The tartness and acidity of the molasses immediately makes you pucker, and naturally we wanted to bottle that up so we could enjoy more of it. This cocktail brings the brightness and flavor of pomegranate molasses, toning down the tartness with sweet pomegranate juice and tonic water. It's the perfect drink for Yalda, the celebration of the winter solstice, when we typically stay up all night reading poetry and eating pomegranates.

Serves 1

—

3 Tbsp pomegranate
   molasses

1 Tbsp granulated sugar

3 Tbsp pomegranate juice

3 Tbsp vodka

Ice cubes, for shaking

1 cup (240 ml) tonic water

Pour 1 Tbsp of the pomegranate molasses onto a saucer or small plate and put the sugar onto a second saucer or small plate. Dip the rim of a tall drinking glass into the pomegranate molasses, spinning it all the way around to coat it evenly, then dip the glass into the sugar, again spinning it around to get an even coating of sugar.

In a cocktail shaker, combine the remaining 2 Tbsp of pomegranate molasses with the pomegranate juice and vodka. Fill the shaker with ice, seal it, and shake vigorously for 10 seconds, or until the cocktail shaker is ice cold to the touch. Strain into the sugar-rimmed glass, then add tonic water to fill the glass. Serve immediately.

SUMAC SMASH VGN · GF

Sumac is typically reserved for sprinkling on top of rice and kabobs, but its brightness can be utilized in so many creative ways, including salad dressings, marinades, and even drinks. It took a decent amount of trial and error to figure out the best way to make a sumac cocktail—it can't just be stirred into a drink, and too much sumac can end up tasting bitter. The solution was a sumac simple syrup, which we love using in our take on a whiskey smash. Combined with fresh mint, lime juice, and whiskey, it makes for an unexpected and fun cocktail that's well suited for a mezze happy hour or a dinner party.

Serves 1
——

SUMAC SIMPLE SYRUP
⅓ cup (65 g) granulated
   sugar
3 Tbsp sumac

SUMAC SMASH
1 lime, halved, with 1 wedge
   reserved for garnish
¼ tsp sumac
4 fresh mint leaves
3 Tbsp whiskey
Ice cubes, for shaking

To make the sumac syrup:
In a small saucepan, bring the sugar and 1 cup (240 ml) of water to a rolling boil over high heat, occasionally stirring with a wooden spoon. When the sugar is completely dissolved, remove from the heat and stir in the sumac. Let cool for 15 minutes, then use a fine-mesh strainer, a coffee filter, or a cheesecloth to strain the sumac out of the syrup. It's okay if there are tiny flecks of sumac left in the syrup!

To make the sumac smash:
Run a lime wedge halfway or all the way around the rim of a coupe. Reserve the lime wedge for garnish. Put the sumac onto a saucer or small plate. Dip the rim of the glass in the sumac, spinning it to coat it evenly.

In the bottom of a cocktail shaker, muddle the remaining lime and the mint for about 30 seconds, or until you can smell the mint and the lime are smashed. Add 1 Tbsp of the sumac syrup and the whiskey. Fill the cocktail shaker with ice, seal it, and shake vigorously for 10 seconds, or until the cocktail shaker is ice cold to the touch. Strain into the sumac-rimmed glass and serve immediately.

CARROT JUICE FLOAT (AB HAVIJ BASTANI) VEG · GF

My parents were very excited to introduce their three highly skeptical children to this Iranian street-food staple. Fortunately, it was love at first sip, the sort of culinary experience that you can't knock until you've tried it. Vanilla ice cream or our Semi-Homemade Saffron and Pistachio Ice Cream (page 196) takes fresh carrot juice to the next level—it's like a Creamsicle that isn't too sweet. This drink is basically a dessert, and we recommend surprising your loved ones with this at the end of a meal. You might face some hesitancy at first, but soon you'll have a table of empty glasses.

Serves 2

——

2 cups (480 ml) good-quality
  carrot juice, cold
2 large scoops good-quality
  vanilla ice cream or
  Semi-Homemade Saffron
  and Pistachio Ice Cream
  (page 196)

Pour the cold carrot juice into two tall glasses, filling them about three-quarters of the way, so the floats don't overflow. Gently place scoops of ice cream into the glasses and serve immediately with straws and long spoons.

Desserts

Rosewater Whipped Cream
VEG · GF — 180

Maman's Peach Muffins
VEG — 183

Soft Almond Flour Cookies (Toots)
VGN · GF — 184

Rosewater and Cardamom Pudding (Masghati)
VEG · GF — 187

Crispy Egg Yolk and Walnut Cookies (Noon Tokhmorgi)
VEG · GF — 188

Sweet Rose and Rice Flour Custard (Fereni)
VEG · GF — 191

Sweet Yogurt Fritters (Noon Masti)
VEG — 192

Syrupy Semolina Cake (Cake-e Sharbati)
VEG — 195

Semi-Homemade Saffron and Pistachio Ice Cream (Bastani Sonnati)
VEG · GF — 196

Mona's Hazelnut Tahini Rolls
VEG — 199

ROSEWATER WHIPPED CREAM VEG · GF

Iranian baked goods have a heavy French influence—it's not uncommon to go to an Iranian bakery and see choux buns, Napoleons, and eclairs behind the counter. Some bakeries spike their whipped cream with a touch of rosewater, which makes for an incredible cake topper or filler, but is also excellent with fresh fruit, Rosy Pancakes (page 40), or Orange and Cardamom French Toast (page 39) for a fun brunch.

If you have time, chill the whisk of your mixer and the bowl in the refrigerator for 30 minutes before making whipped cream. It will still be delicious if you skip this step, but chilling helps the cream whip up faster and fluffier.

Serves 4

———

1 cup (240 ml) chilled
   heavy cream
2 to 3 Tbsp confectioners'
   sugar
2 Tbsp rosewater
Fresh fruit, for serving
   (optional)

In the bowl of a stand mixer fitted with the whisk attachment or a large bowl if using a hand mixer, combine the heavy cream and 2 Tbsp of the confectioners' sugar to start. Whip on medium speed until the cream starts to thicken but before any peaks form, then taste it for sweetness and add more confectioners' sugar as needed, along with the rosewater. Continue whipping on medium speed until stiff peaks form.

Serve immediately, ideally alongside fresh fruit like strawberries, blueberries, and raspberries.

MAMAN'S PEACH MUFFINS VEG

These fruity muffins are soft, sweet, syrupy goodness that can be made year-round thanks to canned peaches. The super simple recipe is a crowd-pleaser and can also be made in a loaf pan or a cake pan, but we've found that muffins plump up with crispy tops and hold up well to pouring peach syrup over the top at the very end of baking.

Makes 12 muffins

———

1 cup (200 g) granulated
   sugar
3 large eggs
1 cup (240 ml) vegetable oil
2 tsp vanilla extract
1½ cups (210 g) all-purpose
   flour
½ tsp baking powder
One 15 oz (425 g) can sliced
   peaches in light syrup
Confectioners' sugar, for
   serving (optional)

Preheat the oven to 350°F (180°C). Line a standard muffin tin with paper liners.

In the bowl of a stand mixer fitted with the paddle attachment or in a large bowl if using a hand mixer, combine the granulated sugar and eggs and beat for about 3 minutes, or until light and fluffy. Add the oil and vanilla and beat until combined.

In a small bowl, use a wooden spoon to stir the flour and baking powder together. Slowly add the flour mixture to the egg and sugar mixture and use the wooden spoon to very gently combine, trying not to stir it more than ten times, so the cake doesn't become dense. Using an ice cream scoop or ladle, scoop the batter into the prepared muffin tin.

Set a fine-mesh strainer over a bowl and drain the peaches, reserving both the peaches and their syrup. Set the syrup aside.

On a cutting board, hold one end of a peach slice and make three lengthwise cuts upward toward the top, without cutting through the end, to keep the peach segment intact and create a fan-like shape. Repeat with the remaining peaches. Fan the slices out and place each peach fan on top of the batter in the muffin cups.

Bake the muffins for 35 to 40 minutes, or until the edges of the muffin tops are light brown. Let the muffins cool for 5 minutes, then pour about 1 Tbsp of the reserved peach syrup on top of each muffin.

Serve the muffins warm or let them cool and top with confectioners' sugar, if desired.

SOFT ALMOND FLOUR COOKIES (TOOTS) VGN · GF

Toots are popular Nowruz cookies—like Christmas, Iranian New Year has its own special cookies and confections that families prepare together around the holiday. I grew up rolling these precious, melty treats with Maman and Maman Bozorg each year. *Toot* means "mulberry" and the name refers to the shape of the cookies. They require no baking, which makes them almost feel like eating cookie dough.

Makes approximately 30 toots

1¼ cups (150 g) blanched slivered almonds

1 cup (120 g) confectioners' sugar

2 Tbsp rosewater

¼ cup (50 g) granulated sugar

Gel food coloring (optional)

Slivered pistachios or almonds, for decorating

If you're using blanched slivered almonds, put them in a food processor and pulse a few times to break them up. Let the food processor run for about 5 minutes, or until you have an almond paste resembling marzipan. Transfer the paste to a medium bowl. Add the confectioners' sugar and use a rubber spatula to combine. Gradually add the rosewater, little by little, and slowly and gently knead, so the dough just comes together. Put the dough in a resealable plastic bag or an airtight container and let it rest at room temperature for 30 minutes.

Pour the granulated sugar into a small bowl and set aside.

After the dough has rested, if you want to dye it with gel food coloring, divide it according to how many colors you're using, and make sure you keep the dough covered, so it doesn't dry out. Wearing gloves to avoid stains, flatten the dough onto a tray or platter. Put a small amount of gel on the tip of a knife, add it to the dough, and very gently knead the dough to distribute the color throughout. If you need more food coloring, add it in small amounts, gently kneading it through, so the dough doesn't get too moist and sticky.

After dyeing the dough, or after your undyed dough has rested, shape your toots. Using your hands, pinch a ½ in (13 mm) size ball from the dough and roll it into an oblong shape (like a mulberry or blackberry), using your fingers to press and pinch the dough into the right shape.

Press a slivered pistachio or almond into the top or bottom side of each toot. One by one, place the toots in the sugar and roll them around to coat. Repeat until you've used all the dough.

Arrange the toots on a platter and serve alongside warm tea. Toots will keep in an airtight container in the refrigerator for up to 1 week.

ROSEWATER AND CARDAMOM PUDDING (MASGHATI) VEG · GF

Maman describes masghati as the type of dessert you whip up if you have a friend coming over at the last minute. I describe it as a spiced, crunchy gelatin treat. Most Iranian households have rice flour, cornstarch, sugar, oil, and butter readily available, so it relies on pantry staples and comes together in about 15 minutes. If you prefer, you can decorate with slivered pistachios instead of almonds.

Serves 4

———

½ cup (70 g) cornstarch

4 cups (960 ml) cold water

1 cup (200 g) granulated sugar

¼ cup (60 ml) rosewater

⅓ cup (40 g) toasted slivered almonds, plus more for garnish

1 Tbsp unsalted butter

¼ tsp cardamom

Pinch of saffron, bloomed in 1 Tbsp boiling water (optional)

In a medium pot, combine the cornstarch and cold water and stir until no lumps remain. Put the pot over medium-high heat and stir constantly with a wooden spoon for roughly 10 minutes, or until the mixture comes to a boil. Turn the heat to low and continue stirring for 5 to 7 minutes, or until the mixture becomes clear and jelly-like. Add the sugar, rosewater, almonds, butter, and cardamom and continue stirring for another 5 to 7 minutes, or until the mixture congeals again. The masghati is ready when a spoon dragged along the bottom leaves a gap in the pan.

Pour the warm masghati into a few small bowls or two larger platters and let cool. If you'd like to decorate your masghati with saffron, save some masghati in the pan and slowly stir in the bloomed saffron, mixing constantly until you achieve your desired hue. Place small spoonfuls of the saffron masghati on top of the bowls and platters of masghati. Decorate the masghati with additional slivered almonds and serve. Masghati will keep in the refrigerator for 5 days.

CRISPY EGG YOLK AND WALNUT COOKIES (NOON TOKHMORGHI) VEG · GF

This is another Nowruz cookie that requires very few ingredients, but calling it a cookie doesn't quite feel right. It's more like a crisp meringue. It was also my great-grandmother's specialty. Every Nowruz, she and her sisters got together to make hundreds of these over the course of an entire day. These family members didn't have electricity, so they beat the eggs by hand, which was tiring and time-consuming, and then baked them in a wood-burning tanoor oven—*tanoor* is the Iranian word for tandoor. Parchment paper wasn't commonly used back then, so they lined copper trays with old newspapers instead. I visualize these women and this process every time I make these treats, feeling gratitude for this recipe—and electric mixers!

Makes about 20 cookies

———

3 large egg yolks

3 Tbsp confectioners' sugar

½ tsp vanilla extract

½ tsp ground cardamom

3 Tbsp finely chopped
   walnuts

Preheat the oven to 350°F (180°C). Line a baking sheet with parchment paper.

In the bowl of a stand mixer fitted with the paddle attachment or in a large bowl if using a hand mixer, beat the egg yolks on medium speed for 3 to 5 minutes, or until the mixture is light in color and elastic. With the mixer on low, gradually add the confectioners' sugar by the spoonful and beat for 1 to 2 minutes, or until fully incorporated. Add the vanilla and cardamom and continue mixing for 30 seconds. With a wooden spoon, gently stir in the walnuts.

Grab the batter little by little, in roughly 2 tsp increments, and place small cookie drops on the parchment paper–lined baking sheet. Bake for 10 to 12 minutes, or until the cookies puff up. The bottoms of the cookies should be a very light brown—if they are darker than that, they're overbaked. Let the cookies cool completely on the baking sheet before serving. Noon tokhmorghi will keep in an airtight container in the refrigerator for up to 1 week.

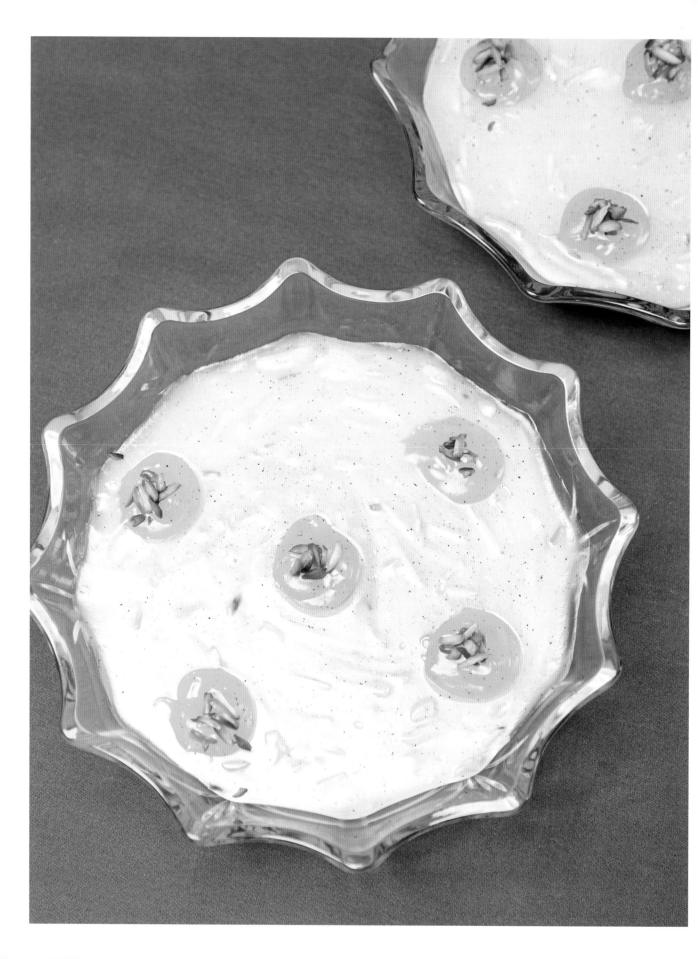

SWEET ROSE AND RICE FLOUR CUSTARD (FERENI) VEG · GF

This delicate, sweet custard feels like a warm hug. Rice flour thickens a milk, rose, and cardamom base, transforming it into a fragrant dessert that can be served warm (my favorite!) at room temperature, or cold, and with a variety of toppings. Our go-tos are pistachios and sour cherry jam, but shredded coconut, any finely chopped nuts, or even a dash of cinnamon are great.

Serves 4

———

2 cups (480 ml) whole milk

2 Tbsp rice flour

2 Tbsp granulated sugar, plus more as needed

1 Tbsp rosewater

2 cardamom pods

Slivered pistachios, for serving (optional)

Fruit jam, for serving (optional)

In a small pot, combine the milk, rice flour, sugar, rosewater, and cardamom over medium heat and cook, stirring constantly with a wooden spoon, for 5 minutes, or until starting to thicken. Taste the custard and add another 1 to 2 Tbsp of sugar, as needed. Continue cooking until the custard is so thick that you can see the bottom of the pan while stirring—this should take roughly 15 to 20 more minutes.

Remove the pot from the heat. The mixture might seem a little runny, but it will thicken further as it cools. Pour the fereni into one medium serving bowl or four small cups and let cool for 10 to 20 minutes to serve warm. Alternatively, you can let the fereni cool to room temperature or enjoy it cold.

Top the fereni with slivered pistachios and/or fruit jam, if desired, before serving. Fereni will keep in the refrigerator for 5 days.

SWEET YOGURT FRITTERS (NOON MASTI) VEG

While writing this cookbook, Maman and I negotiated (sometimes politely, sometimes not) which recipes were essential to include. My mom recalled this recipe late in the process and made it on the spot from a thirty-year-old handwritten recipe. I was immediately convinced, and we haven't found any other version of this recipe out there. This is the Sadeh family recipe for noon masti, fluffy, fried dough coated in confectioners' sugar. The addition of yogurt tenderizes the gluten in the dough, making a soft and light treat that goes perfectly with chai.

Makes 36 fritters

———

2 large eggs

1½ cups (360 ml) vegetable oil

1 cup (240 g) Greek yogurt

1 cup (200 g) granulated sugar

1 tsp baking powder

1½ to 2 cups (210 to 280 g) all-purpose flour

1 cup (120 g) confectioners' sugar

¼ tsp ground cardamom

In a large bowl, whisk together the eggs, ½ cup (120 ml) of the oil, yogurt, granulated sugar, and baking powder. Using a wooden spoon, gradually stir in 1½ cups (210 g) of the flour. Use your hands to knead the mixture for a few minutes into a smooth dough. If your mixture does not come together and feels a little loose, add more flour, 1 Tbsp at a time, and continue kneading it with your hands. When the dough is smooth, soft, and not sticky, loosely cover the bowl with a kitchen towel and let rest at room temperature for 2 hours.

On a lightly floured surface, use a rolling pin to roll out the dough into a large round that is about ½ in (13 mm) thick. Invert a small cup on the outer perimeter of the dough, placing only half of the cup on the dough before pressing down to cut the dough and create crescent-like shapes (not rounds). Arrange the crescent-shaped pieces on a tray and continue the process, rerolling the dough scraps as needed, until you've used all the dough.

Fill a medium Dutch oven with enough of the remaining 1 cup (240 ml) of oil to come about 1 in (2.5 cm) up the sides. Line a tray with paper towels. Warm the oil over medium heat for about 3 minutes, or until a small piece of dough dropped in bubbles up and turns golden.

Working in batches, fry the dough crescents, flipping once, for about 2 minutes per side, or until light brown all over. Use a slotted spoon to transfer the noon masti to the paper towel–lined tray and let cool to room temperature.

In a large bowl, whisk together the confectioners' sugar and cardamom.

In batches, toss the cooled noon masti in the cardamom sugar until evenly coated. Serve warm or on room temperature on a platter, refreshing with cardamom sugar if needed. Noon masti will keep in the refrigerator for up to 1 week or in the freezer for up to 1 month.

SYRUPY SEMOLINA CAKE (CAKE-E SHARBATI) VEG

This cake, often paired with a glass of milk, was Maman's favorite after-school snack and kept her full until dinnertime. It's syrupy but not soggy, with a nice bite from walnuts and lots of floral flavors from rosewater and cardamom. The syrup soaks in the longer the cake sits, making delicious leftovers for an indulgent breakfast or a tasty pick-me-up with chai on the side.

Makes one 9 x 13 in (23 x 33 cm) cake, serves 15 to 20

—

1 cup (240 ml) any dairy or plant-based milk

¾ cup (180 ml) vegetable oil

1¼ cups (250 g) granulated sugar

1 tsp baking powder

1 tsp ground cardamom

1 cup (80 g) unsweetened shredded coconut

2 cups (320 g) semolina flour

½ cup (60 g) chopped walnuts

2 Tbsp rosewater

Preheat the oven to 350°F (180°C). Butter a 9 x 13 in (23 x 33 cm) baking dish.

In a large bowl, whisk together the milk, oil, ¾ cup (150 g) of the sugar, the baking powder, and cardamom until fully combined. Add the shredded coconut, semolina flour, and walnuts and gently whisk until evenly combined. Pour the cake batter into the prepared baking dish, flattening the top evenly with a spatula. Bake for 30 minutes, or until a toothpick inserted into the center comes out clean.

Meanwhile, in a small saucepan, bring the remaining ½ cup (100 g) of sugar and ⅓ cup (80 ml) of water to a boil over high heat. Continue boiling until the sugar is dissolved. Remove from the heat and stir in the rosewater.

When the cake is out of the oven, set the oven's broiler to low. Place the cake under the broiler for 3 to 5 minutes, or until the top turns lightly golden but doesn't burn—watch it closely. Let the cake cool slightly, for about 15 minutes, then use a large spoon to pour the syrup on top of the cake, getting it into the corners and down the sides of the cake. Let the cake absorb the syrup and continue cooling for at least 2 hours before removing from the pan.

Cut the cake into diamond-shaped slices and serve. Semolina cake keeps in the refrigerator for up to 5 days or in the freezer for up to 2 months.

SEMI-HOMEMADE SAFFRON AND PISTACHIO ICE CREAM (BASTANI SONNATI) VEG · GF

Whenever Maman entertains a big group, saffron and rose ice cream laced with pistachios and chunks of frozen cream is her final performance, and it is a showstopper. Making ice cream from scratch is cumbersome, so she figured out a brilliant hack: Use good store-bought pistachio ice cream as the base and mix all the flavors of home right in. Maman's favorite brand to use is Ben & Jerry's—she loves that their pistachio flavor isn't dyed green and that there are full pistachios strewn throughout. She likes to add salep powder (found in Southwest Asian grocers), which gives the ice cream its signature elastic stretch, and serves it with wafer sheets (found in European and Southwest Asian grocers) to make ice cream sandwiches.

Serves 4

½ cup (120 ml) heavy cream

1 pint (480 ml) good pistachio ice cream

2 Tbsp rosewater

¼ to 1 tsp ground saffron, depending on the quality

¼ tsp ground cardamom

1 tsp salep powder (optional)

Wafer sheets, for serving (optional)

Prepare the frozen cream chunks several hours or days before serving: Pour the heavy cream into a small baking sheet to create a ½ in (13 mm) layer. Cover and put in the freezer for at least several hours and ideally overnight.

Move the pint of ice cream from the freezer to the refrigerator 1 to 2 hours before you want to make the ice cream.

In a medium bowl, use a spoon to combine the rosewater, saffron, cardamom, and salep powder (if using). If the liquid is pale yellow, add more saffron, a pinch at a time, and stir until the liquid is a deep red. Add the softened ice cream (reserve the container) and use a rubber spatula to fold the saffron liquid into the ice cream, pulling it through until the ice cream is uniformly golden in color.

Remove the frozen cream from the freezer and use a spoon or knife to break it into small chunks. (If you have trouble getting the frozen cream out, fill a larger container or bowl with hot water and place the frozen container inside to loosen it up.) Add the chunks of frozen cream to the ice cream and quickly fold it through until evenly distributed, so the mixture doesn't melt.

Return the ice cream to its original container (or a new one) and freeze for several hours.

When ready to serve, scoop the ice cream into bowls, or if you have wafer sheets, use scissors to cut them into squares for a traditional Iranian ice cream sandwich. The ice cream keeps in the freezer for up to 1 month.

DESERTS

MONA'S HAZELNUT TAHINI ROLLS VEG

This recipe comes from our dear friend Mona Mohseni. Mona was one of the kindest people and one of the most brilliant chefs we knew—the kind of person who would make homemade bread and yogurt for an afternoon snack or happily prepare a delicious five-course meal for any of her loved ones. Mona's life was tragically cut short in 2021, before the cookbook she was working on (*Caspian*) could see the light of day. Her desire to preserve family recipes and invent new ones inspired by Iranian traditions is the very essence of what *Maman and Me* is about. This book would be incomplete without a tribute to her.

Makes 8 rolls

——

HAZELNUT PASTE
1 cup (140 g) raw
    blanched hazelnuts
1 Tbsp tahini
2 Tbsp unsalted butter,
    melted
1 cup (120 g) confectioners'
    sugar
¼ tsp ground cinnamon
¼ tsp fine salt

DOUGH
1 cup (240 ml) whole
    milk, warm
2¼ tsp (1 sachet) active
    dry yeast
4 Tbsp (55 g) unsalted
    butter, melted
¼ cup (50 g) granulated
    sugar
1 large egg
1 tsp vanilla extract
3 cups (420 g) all-purpose
    flour
½ tsp fine salt

GLAZE
2 cups (240 g) confectioners'
    sugar
3 Tbsp heavy cream
1½ tsp tahini

GARNISH
2 oz (55 g) dark chocolate,
    shaved
1 tsp sesame seeds

To make the hazelnut paste:
In a food processor, process the hazelnuts and tahini for 3 to 4 minutes, or until they form a smooth paste. Add the melted butter, confectioners' sugar, cinnamon, and salt and process for 1 more minute. Slowly add 2 Tbsp of water to thin out the paste, and blend until it is the consistency of peanut butter. Set aside.

To make the dough:
In the bowl of a stand mixer, combine the warm milk and yeast and let sit for about 10 minutes, or until the mixture forms bubbles.

Add the melted butter, granulated sugar, egg, and vanilla to the stand mixer. Using the dough hook attachment, mix on medium speed for about 2 minutes. Add the flour, 1 cup (140 g) at a time, and mix until combined, then add the salt. Continue mixing, occasionally scraping the sides of the bowl with a spatula, until the dough is smooth and sticks to the bottom of the bowl. Transfer the dough to a lightly buttered bowl, cover with a towel, and let rise in a warm and dry place for about 1 hour, or until doubled in size.

continues →

MONA'S HAZELNUT TAHINI ROLLS

Turn the dough out onto a floured surface and use a rolling pin to roll out into a 12 x 16 in (30.5 x 40.5 cm) rectangle, with the long side facing you. Spread the hazelnut paste over the dough, leaving a ¼ in (6 mm) border around the edges. Brush the edges with water and roll the dough away from you into a tight log.

Preheat the oven to 350°F (180°C). Butter a 9 in (22 cm) round cake pan or cast-iron skillet.

Cut the log crosswise into eight pieces. Place the rolls in the buttered pan, then cover with a kitchen towel and let rise for 30 to 45 minutes, or until roughly doubled in size. Bake for 25 minutes, or until the edges of the rolls are golden brown.

To make the glaze:
In a medium bowl, whisk together the confectioners' sugar, heavy cream, and tahini until smooth. While the rolls are still warm, drizzle with the glaze.

To garnish:
Let cool slightly. Top with the chocolate shavings and sesame seeds. The rolls will keep in an airtight container in the refrigerator for 2 days and are best reheated in the oven.

Acknowledgments

I want to start by acknowledging all the family members, loved ones, and ancestors who are no longer living with us—a part of our family and a part of you live on through the recipes and stories in this book.

To Maman Bozorg: I wish you could be here to see this book and to share in this special moment. I miss you all the time, and I think you would be so delighted by this entire project.

To Maman: There is no *Maman and Me* without you and there is no me without you. Thank you for all the time, effort, energy, love, and support you put into this book. Thank you for your endless patience with me as I asked you at least ten thousand food questions in person, on the phone, on video, and over text. Thank you for being an incredible Maman, always, and for providing such a clear example of what love and support looks and feels like. I hope I can make more of your dreams come true. This is just the start—we'll meet Oprah next!

To Baba: You have worked tirelessly to make a bright future for your family, and your sacrifices will never be lost on me. Thank you for supporting us on this project, giving us ideas and inspiration, and for every history lesson on a dish, ingredient, or Iranian culinary tradition (that I was often too tired to fully absorb and appreciate). I love you.

Elly and Aulia Shariat: Thank you for bearing with us as this entire project took over our lives. I'm endlessly grateful for your support along the way.

Mariane Jang: Thank you to my forever friend, who introduced me to Holly La Due at Princeton Architectural Press, changing my life through an email.

Holly La Due: From our first phone call I knew I wanted to work with you. Thank you for fulfilling one of my biggest dreams and thank you for being such a brilliant and kind person to work with.

Thank you to the entire team at PA Press for supporting us, our vision, and our work.

Farrah Skeiky: I couldn't imagine working with anyone else on this beast of a project and having as much fun. Thank you for your patience, your creativity, and your hard work that resulted in these stunning photographs. You are a once-in-a-lifetime talent.

Colin Joon: There is no better partner I could have on this adventure and the adventure of our lives. Thank you for being the first reader, thank you for cheering me on and pushing me further, and thank you for the endless love you've shown me. I love you.

Mallory Pendleton and Laura Buccieri: You were the first people to read my book proposal and your feedback sent me into the stratosphere. Thank you for being phenomenal friends, incredible readers, and such smart writers.

Ariana Feizi: You have encouraged me to write since we were teenagers. This isn't the blog you told me to start, but I think it might be better.

Julia Turshen: Your cookbook writing class helped me write a book proposal and guide the organization of this book. Thank you!

Beyoncé: Your music is the backing force in everything I do. Thank you for blessing us with *Renaissance* while I was in the throes of finalizing this manuscript.

Oprah: Thank you for providing one hour of uninterrupted Maman-and-me time every day you were on air. Maman and I love you so much.

Fig: Your adorable presence in my life has brought me so much joy and love that it needs to be stated here.

To all the friends who tested recipes, cheered me on, shared interest in this project, or are reading this right now: I love you. Thank you for being part of this journey. I'm so grateful to have you along for the ride.

Index

Note: Page references in *italics* indicate photographs.

ROYA SHARIAT is a Brooklyn-based writer and social-impact professional. She has worked for leading brands and nonprofits, including Chobani, Glossier, and the Rockefeller Foundation. Shariat writes a newsletter on food and culture called *Consumed* and runs a popular food TikTok with her mother, Gita Sadeh.

GITA SADEH is a Maryland-based chef and early childhood educator. She has over five decades of culinary experience and more than four decades of teaching experience. Sadeh is known for her cooking online and off—she has catered events and gatherings from her home kitchen and taught Iranian cooking classes to families throughout the DC metropolitan area. Her tens of thousands of fans on TikTok call her "the CEO of tahdig."